INTERNATIONAL LAW

AND

WORLD REVOLUTION

mgen

INTERNATIONAL LAW

AND

WORLD REVOLUTION

by EDWARD McWHINNEY

Professor of Law,
Director, Institute of Air and Space Law,
McGill University, Montreal

A. W. SIJTHOFF | LEYDEN | 1967

Université d'Ottawa
Social Sciences Sociales
University of Ottawa

KZ
3275
.M38
A35
1967

Library of Congress Catalog Card Number: 67-28958

© A. W. Sijthoff's Uitgeversmaatschappij, N.V. 1967 for the World except
Canada

No part of this book may be reproduced in any form by print, photoprint,
microfilm or any other means without written permission from the publisher

Printed in the Netherlands

This book contains the texts of seven half-hour talks first broadcast during December, 1966, and January, 1967, in the radio series *Ideas*. The talks were arranged for the CBC Department of Public Affairs by William Young and produced by Gilles Couture.

To John N. Hazard

AUTHOR'S INTRODUCTION

The within essays were originally presented as a group of public lectures in the *Ideas* series, over the nation-wide network of the Canadian Broadcasting Corporation, in December, 1966, and January, 1967. For purposes of publication in permanent, book form, it has been thought preferable to retain the original style of the lectures as much as possible, rather than to try to render them in the more traditional (usually heavily foot-noted and documented) format of academic publications. What is lost, thereby, in terms of completeness and exhaustiveness of reference to source materials and in terms of acknowledgment and citation of existing authorities in the field, may be compensated for, in some part, by the extra directness of approach particularly from the viewpoint of the non-specialist reader.

My thanks are due to William A. Young, to Janet Somerville, and to J. A. Gonsalves, of the CBC Toronto offices, and to Gilles Couture of the CBC, Montreal, whose kind cooperation and assistance facilitated the delivery and publication of the lectures. Finally, Meriam Matz and Margit Abelsson of the Institute staff, in the McGill University Law School, in Montreal, typed all of the manuscript for publication and otherwise assisted in its preparation.

CONTENTS

The "Old" and the "New"

It is trite, by now, to say that we all live, today, in a revolutionary age. In a sense, of course, the whole of recorded history has been a process of revolution or at least of change, for in no one era has mankind stood completely still. Even the mediaeval "Dark Ages" contained within them the seeds of the later Renaissance and the Reformation, after all.

What characterises the present era, however, and differentiates it sharply from earlier periods of historical development, is the very range and extent and intensity of the changes and the fact that they are occurring now on so many fronts. One has, in this regard, to accept the fact that we are dealing with a World revolution that is really a series of continuing revolutions, finding outlets in numbers of different, if complementary, ways.

The first great revolution of our time, completing a process begun with the outbreak of World War I in 1914 and the subsequent downfall of the old dynasties and empires of Central and Eastern Europe, is what Marxist legal scholars like to identify as the "downfall of Imperialism". This began, of course, with the October Revolution of 1917 and the overthrow of the old Czarist régime in Russia, and was followed up, after the Central Powers' military defeat in 1918, by the abdications of the Sultan of Turkey, the Emperor of Austria-Hungary, and finally the German Kaiser. More important than the essentially symbolic gestures of the replacement of a Sultan or Emperor by a Republican President, were the political changes effected by World War I in the name of Nationalism, Independence, and Liberalism. In deference to Woodrow Wilson's Fourteen Points, the economically viable and politically stable (if unimaginative), Dual Monarchy of the Habsburgs was replaced by a group of weak and struggling, mutually intransigent, "succession states" whose political difficulties were often gravely complicated by racial and religious minority problems and by territorial boundaries that often sacrificed ethnic-cultural justice to supposed geopolitical "natural frontiers". We will recur, later, to the political legacies, in Europe between the two Wars, of the Carthaginian peace imposed by the victors in a War that was supposed, in another of Woodrow Wilson's inspired phrases, "to end all Wars". Suffice it to say, now, that Woodrow Wilson's proclaimed ideal of national self-determination reached its ultimate consummation, after World War II, with the inauguration of the movements for de-Colonisation, Independence, and Self-Government, on a well-nigh universal scale. Whether effected gracefully, as an act of wise statesmanship with an eye to the future, as with British Prime Minister Attlee's Labour Government's granting of independence to the Indian sub-Continent in 1946, or else conceded reluctantly and only after some extended military test of arms, as with the French recognition of Indo-China under the Geneva Accords of 1954 in the wake of the Dienbienphu military disaster, or the equally belated French acknowledgment of Algerian independence, or even not yet conceded at all as with the Salazar government's continuing military resistance to the "national liberation movements" in the Portuguese Colonies in Africa (though not in India, where the Indian government successfully resumed the so-called Portuguese *enclaves* by a unilateral *coup de main*),—the political achievement of de-Colonisation has been the most striking historical development of the two or more decades since the end of World War II. The flood of "new" countries—from Africa, Asia, and the Caribbean—resulting from the effectuation of de-Colonisation has not merely transformed altogether organisations like the United Nations which rested on an original, if shortlived, "victors' consensus" from World War II, but created a vast new arena for competition and interaction of different social and economic systems.

All this, of course, draws attention to the fact that the second great revolution of our time is an ideological one which began, perhaps also, with the Russian Revolution of 1917 and which seemed to reach its climax with the Cold War conflict of the late 1940s and the 1950s; and which has seemed to take a new turn and direction with the burgeoning Russian-Chinese dispute. World War I, again in conventional Marxist dogma, represented the "last working-out of the bourgeois-capitalist system" — supposedly its dying gasp. Of course, the Western-based liberal capitalist system survived that conflict, though undergoing profound internal modifications as a result of the dreadful experiences of the World economic depression of the late 1920s and early 1930s, and the progressive acceptance — in all main Western democratic societies and eventually by all major political parties — of collectivist "Welfare State" ideals of human dignity and social betterment and the community planning techniques that those values implied. When the Iron Curtain finally descended athwart Central Europe, in the late 1940s — thus consolidating and concretising, as an effective political reality, the *de facto* settlements resulting from the German military defeat of 1945 and the Russian military occupation of the Balkans, Eastern Europe, and East Germany (including East Berlin) — and the two rival military blocs faced each other across the ideological frontier, they were each rather different from the theoreticians' erstwhile abstract "ideal-types" or models of 1917 vintage. The West, if it ever had been bourgeois-capitalist in the full sense of the original Marxist theoretical model, had long since evolved into the accepted patterns of the contemporary social democratic planned state. The Soviet Union, for its own part, had moved from the original post-1917 idealistic revolutionary fervour, through the modified capitalistic, N.E.P. revival of the early and middle 1920s, on through Stalin's early era of bureaucratic consolidation and the inauguration of the first of the Five Year Plans, then through the Stalinist Terror of the middle and late 1930s and the great intra-Party purges of the Treason trials, on finally to the undisguised authoritarianism of the dictator's last, paranoiac years, ending with his death in 1953. I shall have more to say, at a later stage in this group of lectures, on the concept of Bipolarity, and the twin military bloc systems — represented in Europe by the rival, though militarily complementary, NATO and Warsaw Pact systems — that provided that political balance of power, or more strictly (in a nuclear age) balance of terror, on which World peace rested, however delicately and precariously, from the time of the break-up of the victorious World War II alliance, very shortly after World War II, until the final achievement of the Kennedy-Khrushchev *détente* with the peaceful resolution of the Cuban missile crisis in October, 1962. Suffice it to say, for the moment, that Bipolarity and the twin military bloc system, projected on a World scale, meant not only a consolidation of political authority within each bloc (including the completion of Soviet political-military hegemony in Eastern Europe by the end of the 1940s), but also a naked struggle for extending of power beyond the post-1945 tacitly accepted spheres of control and influence. This meant not only incessant probing in borderline areas between the two blocs, where the lines of demarcation had not been drawn, once and for all, on a hard and fast basis, — such as in Berlin; and not only mischief-making in "buffer state" areas where internal weakness and irresoluteness or uncertainty of purpose of the other bloc seemed to invite a "fishing expedition" — such as in Korea; but also a continuing propaganda war, and continuing infiltration and internal subversion, in so-called uncommitted countries — in Asia, Africa, and Latin America. As the "winds of change" on these continents brought either de-Colonisation itself, or else widespread social discontent and mass unrest in their wake, they tended to become, in their turn, further battlegrounds for the two opposing blocs; and battlegrounds where, if direct military action or armed attack were, by tacit agreement between the two blocs, excluded, every form of political-psychological pression, propaganda persuasion, and economic blandishment or wooing, was positively included. This was the competition of the ideologies, designed to demonstrate beyond doubt that the one system, rather than the other, could most quickly and effectively advance a developing or "new" country through the early stages of political nationhood and economic growth on to full social and economic well-being for its inhabitants.

At this stage, we approach the third great revolution of our time, which has so radically transformed the contemporary World Community — the revolution as to economic science and technique. In one manifestation, the economic revolution may

4

be viewed as an aspect also of de-Colonisation and the liberation of the former colonial countries from the bonds of economic relations that were linked too narrowly, and certainly too exclusively, to the economic fortunes of the parent, usually European, colonial country. But, beyond this, the economic revolution contends that if the lessons of Keynesian economics and development economics generally are properly accepted and applied, a "new" Afro-Asian country is not condemned by any inexorable laws of economic historical devlopment to a slow, laboured paralleling of the course of the main Western states, over the centuries since feudalism, before it can expect to attain the level of development of these advanced industrial civilisations. The revolution in economic thought preaches that, granted the proper initial development aid in terms of both material resources and also skilled technical advice and counsel, it is possible to escalate quickly through the various stages of economic growth, and, in some cases, to skip certain stages altogether. The revolution in economic thought leaves open the question which of the ways to the advanced industrial society is the most effective — in terms of getting there most quickly, and also perhaps (though this is a highly sophisticated type of enquiry, more likely to be applied in older or declining societies rather than in the more impatient "new" countries) in terms of minimising the deprivations thereby inflicted upon other major community values such as free speech and communication, respect for minority rights, and the like. In a sense the answer to this question, involving in part the decision where to strike the balance between the interests in rapid economic growth and other community values will determine which of the current three main alternative roads to national development and community well-being — Western liberal Capitalist, post-Stalin Soviet Communist, or Chinese Communist — one will opt for. The revolution in economic thought has, so far, also not been able to answer the question of what to do in a World Community where, granted that the lessons of progression through the various stages of economic growth from under-development onwards have been satisfactorily mastered, the gap, in terms of basic standards of living and economic well-being, between the present, advanced industrial societies (both Western Capitalist and European

Communist) on the one hand, and the presently developing countries (Asian, African, Caribbean, and Latin American) on the other hand, is continually widening and accentuating, because of the vastly greater accelerating rate of economic growth of the former. In some respects this ever-widening "margin of misery", cutting across conventional East-West, Communist-Capitalist alignments, and in effect establishing a new North-South alignment in which the economically prosperous and well to do (both European Communist and Western Capitalist) are set in juxtaposition to the economically under-privileged, non-white vast majority of the World's population, is likely to be the politically most explosive element in the World Community for the last third of the century.

The last main revolution in the present era of continuing World Revolution is the revolution in science and technology. In its most dramatic form, this is represented in the inauguration of the nuclear age, and the development of large-scale nuclear weapon technology which has transformed conventional warfare and introduced an uneasy, big-power nuclear "balance of terror" on which World peace now rests—in place of old fashioned political balance of power formations. The spread of nuclear science and knowledge of the techniques and skills of nuclear technology have, however, introduced the new danger of widespread proliferation of nuclear weapons and nuclear irresponsibility on the part of a large host of middle or smaller countries, in place of the nuclear *détente* or tacit understandings as to non-user of nuclear weapons arrived at by the "responsible" nuclear powers—especially the two bloc leaders, the Soviet Union and the United States. This and the progressive weakening of the lines of internal control and authority within each of the two main political-military blocs, in measure as the Soviet-Western *détente* has been concretised and extended, and the danger of a direct, frontal assault between the two bloc leaders largely disposed of, have introduced a new element of instability and uncertainty and unpredictability into international relations that renders urgently necessary the achievement of new and more comprehensive rules and patterns of World public order in a nuclear age. Beyond this, of course, the onset of the Space Age with the massive scientific advances of the post–

6

World War II years, has opened up exciting new challenges and opportunities whose solution seems urgently to demand scientific collaboration in joint programmes transcending the ideological frontiers—in place of the erstwhile isolation which has seen the best scientific man-power in each of the two main ideological systems forced to work in effect in the water-tight compartments established by the political boundaries of the two blocs. The Space Age, even more than the Nuclear Age, seems to offer the dramatic possibility of an International Law of Positive Cooperation in place of the old International Law of Conflict.

.   .   .

We have spoken to date of the Revolution in the World Community—in the society in which international law or any framework and basic patterns of World Public Order must operate. And the question must now be asked, has there been a corresponding revolution in international law and in the juridical concepts of World Public Order? For we teach, in our national Law Schools, of the necessary relation or symbiosis between Law and Society—between positive law rules and prescriptions, as written, and the community in which those same rules are to operate. For without a certain minimum correspondence between the positive law and basic societal facts, the positive law is doomed to remain law-in-books—mere hortatory propositions doomed never to become community "living law". There was a time—particularly in the era between the two World Wars—when national political leaders indulged light-heartedly and incontinently in the poetry of international law-making, and regarded their work as complete when they had elaborated some ideal code of an appropriate high-level of generality and abstraction. The Kellogg-Briand Pact of 1928 to "outlaw War" is a perfect example of just such a casual act of international legislation by simple fiat, without the law-makers bothering too much to concern themselves with the tiresome and irksome underlying causal factors of international tension whose removal or partial alleviation at least could alone give meaning to their high-level declaration and help to make it genuine international law-in-action, as distinct from an ivory tower philosopher's conception of the law-in-books. Today, thank goodness, we are much more pragmatic and empirical, and, if I may say so, modest. And so we teach that any such exercise in abstract, high-level postulation of *a priori* principles, without first studying the underlying problems to which such principles are supposed to relate and indeed to provide a solution, is an exercise in political and legal irresponsibility, the more reckless and cruel and criminal because its political authors know in advance that the high hopes it engenders are likely to turn out to be a cruel deception.

If we look at the corpus of "classical" or traditional international law, today, we find that, on the surface at least and as publicly practised by its main, authoritative interpreters and appliers — *honoratiores* or "dignitaries" of the law, as the great German sociologist, Max Weber, called them — it has little that might be called revolutionary in it. This takes us back to the origins of classical international law itself, and the concept of the international society whose needs and aspirations it was supposed to represent.

It is not so very long since the international society — what we today, in the spirit of universalism, call the World Community — was considered limited, as to the effective participants in international relations among states, to the so-called "civilised nations", these being the Western European or European-derived, essentially Christian, societies that had been founded on the rise of commerce. The fiction was that these countries found their legal personality through their juridical sovereigns or monarchs, and that international law was the expression of their collective consciences. Deference to international law and acceptance of its binding force was effectuated through the principle of comity and the notion of the ethical obligation of each head of state, as a Christian monarch, to give effect to agreements or to commonly observed, customary, rules of conduct. By the opening of the nineteenth century, the membership of the World Community had been expanded, by common consent, to take in a non-Christian society, Turkey. And in the latter half of the nineteenth century, coinciding with the new era of modernisation and Westernisation inaugurated by the Emperor Meiji after 1867, the bounds of the World Community had been stretched to encompass Japan. Everyone else, however, whether nation-state, private association, or individual, while capable of being an object of international law and bound as such by its obligations, was not a subject of international law and hence not entitled as such to claim the benefit of rights deriving from it.

The character and content of classical international law, right to the present day, reflects the ideological narrowness or, if you wish, the essential cultural homogeneity of the members of the original "family compact" in the World Community. For not merely is classical international law rooted in Western legal writings and court decisions and state practice, but its substantive content tends to reflect the complex of interests being pressed by the politically dominant Western societies during the heyday of their commercial and industrial expansion abroad. Some of these rules, it must be said, by their very reasonableness and innate common-sense, have a claim to general acceptance and universality that is marked even at the present day. We might cite, here, the rules making up the modern law of the sea, which, as first developed by the early seventeenth-century Dutch writer, Hugo Grotius, recognise the common interests in free commercial navigation unrestricted by too many or too pressing claims of national sovereignty. It is the Open Seas and a concept of national sovereignty that was limited, at least until the recent Geneva Conferences on the law of the sea, essentially to a three-mile territorial sea, that prevailed over the early Portuguese and Spanish claims to national paramountcy even on the High Seas. Likewise that part of the Law of War known as "temperamenta belli" and devoted to mitigation of the barbarities and cruelties of warfare—again, a concept first sponsored by Grotius and then in direct reaction to the senseless outrages and gratuitous violence of the Thirty Years' War—so obviously corresponds to general interest as to need no further demonstration in terms of inherent rationality.

Nevertheless, the narrowness of the original ideological base for international law, which is the legacy of the historical accident that the original *honoratiores* who so largely created its main substantive rules and principles in its original period of development, were Western European and Christian, is evident. As the respected *Instituto Interamericano de Estudios Juridicos Internacionales* declared, in a joint study prepared in 1964:

> The continuing political and territorial expansion that the European powers so often achieved through military means brought with it and left in its wake a large number of myths. Perhaps the most significant of these was the concept of the inherent universality and perennial nature of international law — a concept that was linked with the old and undefined concepts of natural law. A derivative belief was that *a priori* juridical standards, which could be demonstrated and justified by pure reason and which politically antedated European territorial expansion, governed juridical relations among states . . . . The immanence of a state order was assumed and propositions which historically seemed very closely correlated to the political self-interest of the European powers were accepted as juridical norms.
>
> By their talents and vigour the European peoples extended their influence throughout the world; and Westernisation almost came to be considered as an essential requisite to the achievement of progress. Meanwhile the myth of the immanence and immutability of international law remained unchanged. Even those authors who made studies of the history of international relations *before* the political predominance of the West tended to acknowledge Western Christian standards as the apex of the development of international juridical norms.
>
> The two world wars of this century dispelled these assumptions. The framework of the world changed, and for the modern state the classical international machinery was no longer sufficient . . . Wars were no longer investments in blood and steel made by states to round out their borders or to acquire markets. They were sudden blazes of destruction and hatred which swept away the juridical order — improperly observed, but at least existent — that limited conflicts. Colonial expansion, which no longer had the characteristics of Victoria's days, is another example. Freedom of trade, the protection of nationals abroad, and the propagation of Christianity ceased to be justifications. Christianity was no longer regarded as the only true religion, and all peoples were thought to have the right to live out their destiny without undergoing Westernisation.

The dissatisfaction that so much of the non-Western membership of the contemporary World Community — now expanded from its original, essentially Western European or Western European–derived "family compact" on a basis of well-nigh universality as to colour, race, religion, and ideology — feel, rightly or wrongly, with the corpus of historically-received, "classical" international law that must be applied, now, to solution of present-day problems and tension-issues of international relations, is indicated in varied representative reactions.

For example, the late great Professor Eugene Korovin, at the time the *doyen* of Soviet international lawyers, called in 1961 for the replacement of what he identified as the "routine system" of international law by a new programme that would express the "epoch of struggle between two opposing social systems; the epoch of Socialist revolutions; the collapse of imperialism; the abolition of the colonial system; the transition on to the Socialist road of more and more peoples; and the victory of Socialism and Communism on a world scale".

More recently, the representative of one of the "developing" African countries, at the special United Nations Conference on International Law held at Mexico City in the Fall of 1964, bitterly attacked the Statute of the World Court for its identification (in Article 38(1)(C)) as one of the sources of law that the court is to apply in deciding cases coming before it — of "the general principles of law recognised by civilised nations". This provision, the African governmental representative concerned said, was hardly likely to dispel the "new" countries' general lack of confidence in the World Court.

All this indicates, of course, that there is a fairly widespread crisis of confidence in international law at the present day. For many peoples, particularly in the "new" countries, the corpus of classical, historically-derived, international law not merely provides no affirmative base for satisfying their claims for economic advancement and social betterment for their peoples, but in many respects seems to represent a positive barrier or obstacle against those claims. And organisations like the World Court and the United Nations policy-making organs, which, for most of their history, have seemed to many peoples, particularly in the "new" countries, to be essentially Western-composed, or Western-influenced or dominated, have seemed too often to be preoccupied with the petit-point needlework of international law, rather than to be concerned with its imaginative reshaping and rewriting to meet radically new conditions in international society. The prime task of the international lawyer today in a World Community undergoing continuing revolution, becomes, therefore, one of building a new system of World Public Order with an ideological base broad enough to derive support from, and to encompass, all the main competing, social and economic

11

systems of the present day; and of developing, in the international arena, that necessary symbiosis between positive law and social change that we regard as axiomatic for our own internal law system in our own national society. In a word, any viable system of World Public Order or international law generally, today, must capture, in measure, the dynamic of the World revolution of our time. How this can best be attempted in a World of ideological differences and conflict will represent the subject matter of the succeeding discussion.

Competing (Communist and Western)
Systems of World Public Order

In a widely-quoted address to the Annual Meeting of the American Society of International Law, in Washington in the Spring of 1963, the former Secretary of State of the United States, Dean Acheson, took as his theme the "quarantine" measures applied by the United States administration during the Soviet-Western crisis of October, 1962, to ensure the removal of the Soviet offensive, ground-to-ground, nuclear missiles from Cuba. The quarantine measures, in Dean Acheson's view, were:

> . . . not a legal issue or an issue of international law as these terms should be understood. Much of what is called international law is a body of ethical distillation, and one must take care not to confuse this distillation with law. We should not rationalise general legal policy restricting sovereignty from international documents composed for specific purposes . . . .
>
> I must conclude that the propriety of the Cuban quarantine is not a legal issue. The power, position and prestige of the United States had been challenged by another state; and law simply does not deal with such questions of ultimate power—power that comes close to the sources of sovereignty. I cannot believe that there are principles of law that say we must accept destruction of our way of life . . . . No law can destroy the state creating the law. The survival of states is not a matter of law.

Dean Acheson's remarks call attention, of course, to the fundamental dilemma of international lawyers of the present era, dominated as it is by the political facts-of-life of Big-Power confrontation, and of resultant conflict or cooperation between them, whenever any one of them assumes his own special interests to be threatened. The formal legal structure of contemporary World Public Order — the law-in-books — is still what it was in 1945, that is to say *one World* represented by a United Nations organisation in which all states, large or small, were represented and in which all were subject to the one international law. The realities of the international law-in-action, however, are that once the so-called wartime "alliance against Fascism" had achieved its original purpose with the final military defeat of the Axis powers, and once the victors had begun to quarrel among themselves over the division of the spoils of victory, in Europe and in Asia, the original *one World* premise of the United Nations disappeared. Once the Iron Curtain had fallen across Central Europe, as it had, effectively, within a year after the conclusion of the War in Europe, the *de facto* post-war military settlement of 1945 began progressively to be concretised and ultimately, if you wish, legitimated, with the creation of the twin political-military bloc systems, NATO and the Warsaw Pact, which were each dominated, and largely controlled in the early years, by their respective bloc leaders, the United States and the Soviet Union. The United Nations, whose constitutional structure, at least, had been predicated upon the premise of continuing Big-Power cooperation in the post-war years, found itself transformed into an arena, and not necessarily the most important arena at that, for Big-Power ideological confrontation, and for the struggle for competitive political advantage between the two blocs. In those situations where the two bloc leaders chose to bring their political disputes and differences before the United Nations, the naked power struggle and the continuing pressing for tactical advantages in the Security Council and the General Assembly and the specialised agencies as an aid to the warfare of the ideologies, transformed the whole character of the United Nations. For, as a body conceived of and brought into being along basically classical, Western-derived, constitutional lines, the United Nations' ability to work usefully, and ultimately to survive as an effective political force, depended upon respect for the parliamentary "rules of the game" and for the principles of, at least minimum, intra-organisation cooperation and mutual respect and decency that those involve.

When the two bloc leaders chose *not* to bring their disputes before the United Nations, however (and this became true of an increasing number of major issues), the political by-passing of the United Nations' organisation weakened its political authority and prestige, and inevitably also its efficacy as an arena for international problem-solving. Beyond this the recourse to Big-Power direct action, which the by-passing of the United Nations necessarily involved, encouraged the view that power, and not law, was the decisive element in international problem-solving, and so helped to weaken respect for international law generally, in the post-war World Community.

To look again at the example taken by Dean Acheson as the theme for his exegesis on the relation between Law and Power — the Cuban missile crisis of October, 1962 —, the first most striking fact is that, in a Big-Power, face-to-face ("eyeball to eyeball", in the Kennedy term) confrontation between the two bloc leaders, the United States and the Soviet Union, that brought the World to the edge of full-scale nuclear war, all the significant dealings and negotiations between the two bloc leaders occurred directly, usually in the form of personal exchanges between the two Heads-of-State, President Kennedy and Premier Khrushchev. And the final settlement — the Soviet agreement to withdraw the offensive, ground-to-ground, missiles from Cuba in return (as one understands it) for a tacit American undertaking not to invade Cuba or to try to overthrow Fidel Castro by direct, military means — was achieved in a series of private messages between the two Heads-of-State. To be sure, at a certain stage during the American "quarantine action" against Cuba, the Organisation of American States was brought into the act; but the important fact is that this occurred only *after* President Kennedy and his advisers had decided upon the naval blockade measures. To be sure, also, U.S. Ambassador to the United Nations, Adlai Stevenson, at various stages, gave the United Nations advice concerning American actions and attitudes to the Soviet nuclear investment in Cuba; but Ambassador Stevenson at no time seems to have been crucial, or influential in the U.S. executive decision-making during the Cuban missile crisis, and his various statements, in the U.N. arena, at all times succeeded upon, and in no way seemed to have preceded or shaped, the actual American decision-making.

If we look at the really crucial breakthroughs in international relations in this post-war era, transcending the ideological frontiers on a genuine, inter-systems basis, we tend to find again that they have been achieved outside the United Nations arena, and usually on a direct, person-to-person, basis between the two bloc leaders, the United States and the Soviet Union. One understands that Premier Khrushchev of the Soviet Union preferred direct, bilateral negotiation with the American Head of State for purposes of resolving East-West major tension-issues, because of a certain distaste for open, public negotiation and the frequent noisiness and playing to the gallery that that involves at the expense, very often, of the business of resolving conflicts. Premier Khrushchev was a man who understood the facts of power, of course. One of his most famous comments upon the international scene is a rebuke to the Albanian political leaders for their "irresponsible" approach to international relations in the nuclear era. As Premier Khrushchev said:

> To use a familiar expression: 'blessed is he who jabbers about war without knowing what he is talking about'. The Albanian leaders talk a lot about rocket and nuclear war, but nobody is worried about their talk. Everyone knows that they have nothing to their name but idle talk and that they have no real possibilities. As you see, our positions on these questions and our responsibilities are different.

Premier Khrushchev, as a colourful man with a keen tactical sense, was not above using an international forum like the United Nations to score propaganda points: his celebrated shoe-banging episode, in the United Nations General Assembly, was an example of his bold and imaginative, if somewhat crude, skill in capturing newspaper headlines in a conceived national propaganda interest. But Premier Khrushchev also had a certain feeling for the choice of the right time and the right occasion; and he recognised therefore that one should not confuse an occasion for propaganda-making with an occasion for actual problem-solving. When it came to problem-solving, his view was that the really serious business of resolving Soviet-Western conflicts should not be allowed to be obscured or delayed or defeated by having a whole lot of unnecessary, unimportant, and — if you wish — "irresponsible" lesser people around to complicate fundamental bargaining between the two people who alone led from a position of strength and power — the two bloc leaders, the United States and the Soviet Union.

Premier Khrushchev's preferences on this point as to the *method* of resolving fundamental Soviet-Western conflicts, seem to have been shared by American political leaders, in the Kennedy administration years at least, in reaction to the talkativeness and sheer capriciousness of so many State representatives in the greatly expanded U.N. General Assembly of recent years. As a result of this coincidence of U.S. and Soviet views on the choice of arenas for resolving fundamental international conflicts, the Kennedy-Khrushchev era was characterised by the preference for the private Summit Meeting *à deux* of the U.S. and Soviet Heads-of-State or their immediate personal confidants, as the ultimate refinement in method for maintaining international peace and for international law-making in general. This was the operational methodology employed, after all, for achievement of the Moscow Nuclear Test Ban Treaty of August, 1963; for it was negotiated, and its actual text worked out and agreed upon, in personal talks between the Soviet Foreign Minister, Mr. Gromyko, and President Kennedy's special representative, Mr. Harriman (plus Lord Hailsham of the United Kingdom). It is true that the U.N. Secretary-General, U Thant, was invited to be present at the formal signing of the Treaty in Moscow on August 8th, 1963; but the invitation to him seems to have been more in the nature of a polite afterthought and in any case not to have reflected any actual United Nations contribution to the work leading to the successful conclusion of the Treaty. Likewise, though the Nuclear Test Ban Treaty, after its formal signing in Moscow by the three principals who had actually worked it out, was made open to other states for adherence, and in fact more than a hundred states have since signed it, these lesser states were powerless to change the text of the Treaty and of course in no way had been consulted about, or had contributed to, its final terms.

In measure, one might say the same thing about the recent U.N.-based Treaty on the Peaceful Uses of Outer Space. Though, in contrast to the Moscow Test Ban Treaty, the Space Treaty has, as a formal matter, been handled by a special U.N. Committee; and though individual jurists, outside both the United States and the Soviet Union, have made important contributions (especially the brilliant Polish jurist and chairman of the special

U.N. Committee, Manfred Lachs, who has just been elected to the World Court), the fact remains that the Treaty only became inevitable once — within a day of each other in June, 1966, and with a synchronisation as to timing and drafting that bespeaks months of private bilateral U.S.-Soviet discussions — the U.S. and the Soviet Union submitted substantially identical drafts for a Treaty. The final text of the Space Treaty, agreed upon in December, 1966, is essentially an assimilation and blending of the two drafts, U.S. and Soviet.

Reference to the *method* of resolving international tension-issues and to the current preference of the two bloc leaders for by-passing the United Nations organisation in favour of quiet diplomacy *inter partes,* and of more streamlined, and certainly speedier, machinery for international problem-solving, leads on to the issue of the substantive nature of the conflicts-resolution that is to be made — meaning, here, the actual law to be applied. The Cuban missile crisis of October, 1962, and the role of international law in its actual resolution, have been the subject of continuing discussion and debate in North American legal circles: the 1964 Annual Meeting of the American Society of International Law in Washington, for example, was largely built around this theme. From the American viewpoint, the *political* problem, in the Cuban crisis of October, 1962, — once the facts of the Soviet emplacement of offensive, ground-to-ground nuclear weapons in Cuba had been satisfactorily established by aerial overflights, photographic evidence, intelligence reports, and the like — was to remove what President Kennedy's military advisers assured him was a major disturbance to that Cold War military "balance of power" (more strictly, "balance of terror", in nuclear terms) on which World peace had rested, however precariously, ever since the time of the break-up of the victorious World War II coalition and the establishment of the Iron Curtain athwart Central Europe. We know, now, the gravity of the threat presented to the North American defence system by the clandestine Soviet nuclear incursion into Cuba. For the offensive, ground-to-ground, nuclear weapons, directed from operational military bases in Cuba would have effectively by-passed the tightly organised "Northern Approaches" radar defence network. While a similar, "Southern Approaches" radar defence network did in fact exist, it had never been given the priority accorded to the Northern Screen, for the very simple reason that an attack from the South on Washington, New York, or for that matter Toronto or Montreal, had never figured highly in Western military planners' expectations up to that time — the Fall of 1962. The effect of Premier Khrushchev's "fishing expedition" into Cuba — induced, one understands, by the Soviet military Chiefs of Staff view that they could create a nuclear *fait accompli* undetected by American intelligence, coupled with Premier Khrushchev's own hunch, based on his meeting with President Kennedy in Vienna the year before, that the American President was a weak man who would tolerate even a disturbance of the political-military *status quo* adverse to American interests rather than risk the danger of a nuclear war — would have been to mount a new and massive nuclear threat on America's southern flank, against which no really effective advance warning system existed up to that time. Though Premier Khrushchev's official statements, after his Cuban nuclear ploy had been publicly revealed, all asserted that the attempt to place nuclear weapons in Cuba was an essentially friendly, non-aggressive gesture in aid of a fraternal, Communist country against threats of invasion in the future by the forces of Imperialism (here, the United States), the fact that Premier Khrushchev and his military Chiefs of Staff did not limit themselves to defensive, ground-to-air, missiles, but included, in addition, substantial numbers of purely offensive, ground-to-ground missiles with a range capable of attaining Washington and New York and even Toronto and Montreal, exposed the true purpose of the venture as an attempt, by stealth, to introduce a new nuclear factor into the then existing Cold War military balance of power. I may say, in this regard, that one of the principal counts in the official Soviet governmental denunciation of Premier Khrushchev, on the occasion of his dismissal from office in the Fall of 1964, was his alleged nuclear "irresponsibility" in having ventured so abruptly and cavalierly into a recognised American sphere of political influence, thus threatening the Cold War military *status quo* and provoking, in turn, the risk of a massive American retaliation and escalation into a full-scale nuclear war.

We have been speaking of the *political*, or *political-military* problem presented for the United States and the West by the Soviet clandestine nuclear incursion into Cuba, as being one of a disturbance of the then existing Cold War military balance of power, that had in general, since Stalin's death at least, been tacitly recognised and mutually observed by both the Soviet bloc and the West. There were some people in the United States, perhaps, who wished to characterise the *political* problem more broadly, as being an ideological threat to American political and economic interests in the Americas posed not so much by Premier Khrushchev's nuclear infiltration into Cuba, as by the mere fact of the continued existence of Fidel Castro's Communist régime in Cuba after the abortive U.S.-sponsored, "Bay of Pigs" insurgent landings of April, 1961. To his credit, President Kennedy rejected any such attempt at characterisation of the Cuban crisis in narrowly anti-Castro, anti-Communist terms; but insisted on viewing it in the context of Soviet-Western relations and the maintenance of the East-West *de facto* political-military balance. This meant, on the part of President Kennedy and his advisers, limiting the political-military problem to the situation created, vis-à-vis Hemispheric defence, by the new factor of the Soviet offensive nuclear presence in the Americas, and limiting the political-military solution to the problem, accordingly, to the securing of the removal of the Soviet offensive nuclear weapons from Cuba. It excluded, on this basis, any temptation, to the President, to expand the political-military solution to the problem, so as to make the occasion an excuse, also, for getting rid of Fidel Castro and his government, once and for all, by direct military action.

Once he had characterised the political problem and its preferred political solution, with a restraint that did credit to his calmness and prudence of political judgment, President Kennedy was faced with the problem of choice of the *legal* solution — meaning the particular international law machinery and substantive principles to invoke in support of the action to be taken. In saying this I do not mean to imply that the political and the legal characterisations were separated, temporally, in the act of executive decision-making in the Cuban crisis, with the issue of choice of legal means and legal remedies being looked at only *after* all the crucial policy options had been considered and the final choice arrived at on high political grounds. There are, it is true, some students of the Continental *Realpolitik* school who will always argue that the executive decision-maker makes his choices on a basis of naked power and national interest alone, and *then* calls in his international lawyers to provide polite foot-notes for later historians or for respectable window-dressing for his own, or especially neutral, states' public opinion. Such a cruelly cynical approach leads inevitably to the pre-World War I doctrine of *Kriegsraison* and to a contempt for international law that is captured in the historic phrase of the 1914 Imperial German Chancellor (Bethmann-Hollweg) dismissing the Belgian Neutrality Treaty of 1831 as a "mere scrap of paper". To his credit, President Kennedy never embraced any such doctrine.

Though an historian and not a lawyer by intellectual training, President Kennedy had, nevertheless, a keen feeling for international law and for legal thought-ways in general. And we know that, in the actual process of executive decision-making in the Cuban missile crisis, legal considerations entered into the discussion and policy-planning right from the outset and helped to shape the final result and the final choice of means for resolving the problem. As Professor Abram Chayes of the Harvard Law School, the then Principal Legal Adviser to the State Department, has revealed:

> The confrontation was not in the courtroom and, in a world destructible by man, a legal position was obviously not the sole ingredient of effective action. We were armed, necessarily, with something more substantial than a lawyer's brief. But though it would not have been enough merely to have the law on our side, it is not irrelevant which side the law was on. The effective deployment of force, the appeal for world support, to say nothing of the ultimate judgment of history, all depend in significant degree on the reality and coherence of the case in law for our action.

It is an integral part of the legal process to be concerned with questions of ways and means. And one of the principles that we teach, in our national law schools, is that of economy in the use of power in aid of legal decisions—that is to say, that given a choice between several alternative modes of reaching a given legal result, the legally correct course of action is to adopt that solution that inflicts the least deprivations on other widely-held community values. In a word, one should opt for the more moderate legal controls, where the alternatives rely too heavily on naked power or military direct action as the means of achieving their result. It is in this respect, especially, that President Kennedy's final policy choice to resolve the Cuban missile crisis was *legal* in the best sense of contemporary international law. Rejecting the advice of the "hawks" in his National Security Council advisory group who wanted direct aerial bombing of the Cuban missile bases themselves, to eliminate the missiles and their firing installations, he opted instead for the "quarantine" control device as the measure designed to ensure effective removal of the Soviet offensive nuclear missiles from Cuba *but to do no more than that.* President Kennedy thus avoided the twin dangers that military direct action and a substantial public display of force might have presented — that is, a public humiliation and consequent loss of face for Premier Khrushchev which might have unnecessarily exacerbated Soviet-Western relations for the future; and an irrational Soviet military response, in kind, which could have triggered off a full-scale nuclear war.

It is significant, in this respect, that after the then Soviet Ambassador to the United Nations, Mr. Zorin, had made his initial angry attack in the United Nations (which in any case, was shortlived), the legality of the American actions in the Cuban missile crisis was thereafter not disputed by the Soviet Union. Premier Khrushchev's own ultimate acceptance of the American-applied Cuban "quarantine" measures was, in Walter Lippmann's words, "rather elegant and nonchalant". I have yet to find, in the Soviet scientific legal writings, any contesting by any Soviet jurist of intellectual stature or public standing of the basic legality, in terms of international law, of President Kennedy's actions to resolve the Cuban missile crisis.

But if the legality of the American actions in the Cuban crisis is not being actively contested in *Soviet* legal circles, I have mentioned that that subject is under continuing debate in *American* legal circles. This American discussion and criticism tends to go to a seeming American acquiescence, and indeed sponsorship, in an effective by-passing of the United Nations and of U.N. regionally-based legal machinery, in favour of direct inter-bloc legal dealing; or to a substantial expansion of the old international law category of Pacific Blockade, well beyond the limits which had so far been accepted for it in custom-based international law; or to an interpretation of the ambit of legally permissible "self-defence" which goes well beyond the provisions of Article 51 of the United Nations Charter (if it does not contravert that altogether), and which seems to postulate a common-law right of self-defence separate from and antecedent to the U.N. Charter. Although the United States administration — as the formal ground for justification, in international law, of the legality of its Cuban Quarantine measures — decided to rely principally, if not exclusively, upon regionally-based legal arguments in terms of the U.N. Charter, that looked to the authorisation (in fact, more strictly, subsequent ratification) of the U.S. Administration action by the Council of the Organisation of American States, the debate among American international lawyers over the legal grounds of the Cuban crisis action, does draw attention to some of the main dilemmas of international law in the contemporary World Community.

As a matter of international law-in-action, United Nations-based law cannot be said today to represent one overarching, paramount body of legal principles covering all possible international problems and providing instant, ready-made solutions for them. Instead, international law today, as law-in-action, is really a congeries of separate systems of international law which sometimes operate in separate spheres, sometimes overlap, and sometimes directly conflict or collide. United Nations law is an important part of that congeries of separate international laws, but only a part. In particular, when the fundamental interests of the two main ideological blocs and especially their leaders, the Soviet Union and the United States, clash, it is unrealistic, as a matter of international law-in-action, to expect such vital issues to be resolved in the arena of the United Nations, or to blame the United Nations for having failed, itself, to provide a solution. Our short-term interest, as international lawyers, becomes one of seeing that great international tension-issues are resolved by *legal* means, whether in the United Nations itself or by direct, big-power negotiation in Summit Meetings. Our long-term interest is to try increasingly to persuade the big-powers to avoid the arbitrariness, caprice, and simple chance, of these bilateral dealings, however well-intentioned; and to persuade them to cooperate in institutionalising settlement of international disputes by setting up appropriate machinery for conflicts-resolution in advance of the conflicts actually arising— preferably, of course, in the United Nations itself.

The first interest—that of ensuring that Cold War, nuclear age ideological conflicts are actually resolved, and resolved by legal means—has in fact been achieved in considerable measure already, through all the international *Sturm und Drang* of recent years. The development and increasing concretisation of a species of inter-bloc international law—or Cold War "rules of the game", if you wish—is one of the most striking, and hopeful, phenomena of the era of the Khrushchev-Kennedy *détente* inaugurated by the peaceful resolution of the Cuban missile crisis.

The effectuation of the second interest—that of effectively institutionalising international conflicts-resolution and peace-keeping generally—becomes the prime and urgent obligation of our time, as that old political-military *status quo* and the Cold War balance of power, born of the *de facto* détente between the two ideological blocs and their leaders, the Soviet Union and the United States, is threatened and begins to crumble under the impact of such events as the Chinese challenge to Russia for World Communist leadership; the fission, if not actual break-down, in the erstwhile Western military alliance in Europe; and the rise of the "new" countries of Asia, Africa and Latin America. We have, in the West, learned by now to live with Soviet Communists; and so the weakness in the United Nations and in the official institutions for maintaining and extending World Public Order has not troubled our consciences too much. But we have not yet learned how to cope with the Pandora's Box of problems presented by the imminent threat of wide-scale proliferation of nuclear weapons into "irresponsible" hands, and by the ever-widening "margin of hunger" between the privileged whites (both Communist and Western) in the World and the large mass of under-privileged non-whites. That is why the emphasis on machinery and institutions is of such vital importance.

*The U.N. Security Council and General Assembly
as "Parliament of Mankind"*

The United Nations organisation, as constructed and achieved
at the San Francisco Conference in 1945, was the creation of the
victorious "wartime Alliance against Fascism". By definition,
the defeated Axis Powers did not participate in its creation; nor
did the few remaining neutral countries who outlived the War.
These latter, indeed, when they later came to apply for membership in the United Nations, had to run the political gauntlet
involved in meeting the legal criteria for membership established
under the Charter: the Soviet jurist, Judge Krylov, in a dissenting opinion in the World Court Advisory Opinion of 1948 on
Conditions of Admission of a State to Membership in the United
Nations, suggested that Eire was not a "peace-loving" state, as
stipulated in Article 4 (1) of the Charter as a condition of
membership, because it had not taken part in World War II.
In Judge Krylov's view, to be peace-loving was no mere passive
state of mind, as the terms used in the French text of the Charter
— "Etat pacifique" — might imply: on the contrary, the English
text's "peace-loving", the Spanish text's "amantes de la paz",
and also the Russian and Chinese texts, had a more active sense,
which made "tak(ing) part in World War II alongside the
democratic countries" a relevant criterion for admission to membership in the United Nations.

    The point is, of course, that the United Nations Charter, as
originally conceived and drafted as a blueprint of World Public
Order, was the creation of only a part of the World Community
— the victorious Allies; and, even here, the actual drafting was
the work of a relatively small group of major powers, with the

Soviet Union's rôle, from the beginning, being rather negative and defensive.

Just why the Soviet Union chose to be less than enthusiastic about the embryonic United Nations organisation is not hard to discern. Right from its outset, that earlier experiment in a constitutionalism of World Public Order—the League of Nations —had seemed to Soviet jurists to have a bourgeois-capitalist, Imperialist orientation. At best, it was a legal device or stratagem for preserving, for Lloyd George and the other Western heads of state, the fruits of the Carthaginian Peace Treaty that they had imposed on defeated Imperial Germany at Versailles; at worst, it was a political instrument for containing and defeating the Soviet Union and the other forces of World Revolution of the down-trodden masses. From its establishment in 1919 until the Soviet Union finally opted to join it in September, 1934, the League of Nations was viewed, by Lenin, and then by Stalin, as being an essentially anti-Soviet coalition. In the Soviet Union's brief membership of the League of Nations—from 1934 until its exclusion, by decision of the League, in December, 1939, by reason of the Red Army's invasion of Finland—the Soviet Union had very little reason to be impressed with the operational utility or the effectiveness, as international law-in-action, of this first major attempt at institutionalising World Public Order, along constitutional lines. For, these were the years of the breakdown of Collective Security and the League of Nations' ignominious retreat and weakness in the face of the naked Italian aggression in Ethiopia, and then, increasingly, of the Japanese military penetration of China, and of Nazi Germany's successive repudiations of detailed provisions of the Versailles Treaty in favour of pursuit of its own *irredentist* claims by military threat or direct military action where that failed.

In the case of the United Nations, from its first establishment in 1945, it was clear that the Soviet Union could not hope to command a political majority in it, and so to dominate or control proceedings. At best, by joining, the Soviet Union could prevent the United Nations from becoming a hostile, anti-Soviet, instrument, as (in the Soviet view) the old League of Nations had become effectively, without Russian membership, in the period from its founding in 1919 until 1934. But this was a not unimportant political objective, in itself; and so, once the decision to join had been made, the Soviet Union's objectives, in the actual drafting sessions for the U.N. Charter, became to secure, expressly in the Charter itself, adequate, built-in, institutional-machinery guarantees to protect it against the arbitrary will of political majorities in any of the U.N.'s main organs. This initial, "defensive", conception of the United Nations, on the part of the Soviet Union and its main associates, is the explanation both of some of the main internal contradictions and conflicts in the United Nations' final form, and also of the Soviet Union's general, long-range attitudes to the United Nations as an arena for fundamental Soviet-Western ideological competition, in the first decade and a half, at least, of its existence.

The internal contradictions in the United Nations' constitutional machinery are inherent in the uneasy compromise that it effects between, on the one hand, the philosopher's conception of "One World" and a genuine, universal, "Common Law of Mankind"; and the elemental facts of power of the post-war World, dominated, as it was, by the political system of Bipolarity and the two competing military-ideological blocs (Soviet and Western).

The "One World" concept, of course, is reflected in the whole idea of attempting to institutionalise World public order in constitutional terms; in the implicit concept of universality of membership in the new organization, albeit a universality conditioned legally by the requirement of being "peace-loving"; in the provision for continuing the World Court as the common tribunal of mankind, albeit with a jurisdiction limited by the pre-condition of the voluntary submission of states. Those international lawyers who are also constitutional lawyers will recognise, immediately, some dangers inherent in institutionalised projection of the "One World" concept that is rooted in essentially Western-derived, special constitutional concepts. We know enough, today, of the special space-time dimensions in which basic, modern Western constitutional ideas were conceived to be modest about their chances for survival and growth when exported to other, essentially non-Western societies, as they have been in such large measure, since the War, to the "new" countries of Asia and Africa. Western constitutionalism, after all, as (in Judge Learned Hand's words) "the last flowers of civilisation", may flourish under ideal conditions; but it is crucially dependent, for its survival, on existence and observance of special constitutional "rules of the game", of mutual self-restraint and fairness, and (in Judge Learned Hand's words) that general "spirit of moderation" that tends only to be found in societies that have already achieved their revolutions and so have had time to afford to develop the calmer, more stable, legal values. As an exercise in rationalised constitutionalism, Western style, the United Nations Charter has a resemblance to American constitutional styling and phrasing that is only in measure explained by the use of the American poet, Archibald MacLeish — in 1945, a U.S. Assistant Secretary of State specially seconded to the San Francisco Conference — as an adviser on the final language and drafting. It is important, however, to recognise that the U.N. Security Council and the U.N. General Assembly, like any other, Western-derived or Western-influenced, constitutional organs, are crucially dependent upon observance of the constitutional "rules of the game" for their effective working and indeed for their survival as viable political institutions. Persistent obstructionism or sheer wilfulness and perversity in the face of majority will, along the lines of the "Irish members'" conduct in the pre–World War I British House of Commons or the Southern members' filibuster in the United States Congress, can bring a parliamentary body to a complete standstill and defeat or delay its work: on the other hand, a parliamentary majority that recognises no limits as to the exercise of prudence and self-restraint vis-à-vis minority rights and interests may equally become guilty of contempt for the parliamentary processes and ultimately for constitutional government itself. Both of these conditions, it has been suggested (in different quarters and usually for different reasons), have been strongly in evidence in the work of the United Nations Security Council and General Assembly at various times since 1945.

The deference to the facts of power — here the (in immediate, 1945 terms) incipient condition of Bipolarity in the World Community — actually made in the United Nations Charter, is reflected in the institution of the Big-Power Veto that was specially built into the voting rights and procedures in the

Security Council; and in the practical paramountcy, as to political policy-making powers, given to the consequently Big-Power
dominated Security Council vis-à-vis all other U.N. organs and
especially the General Assembly. As a matter of the law-in-books,
the Veto power was accorded to all the Big-Powers of 1945 — the
original, wartime, "Big Five" — the United States, Soviet Union,
Great Britain, France, and China. As a matter of the law-in-
action, since the other four of the original "Big Five" (China
remaining, of course, Nationalist China even after its retreat
from the mainland in 1948) all represented the same ideological
base and therefore invariably made common cause on major
political issues, it was a matter of the Soviet veto operating in
the Security Council to defeat Western-sponsored decisions or
action of the U.N. There is no doubt that, in the early years of
the United Nations when Stalin was still in power in the Soviet
Union and when the Cold War battle lines were therefore well
drawn, the Soviet veto, many times actually used and many times
merely threatened to compel withdrawal of announced action,
operated to defeat decisions desired by the overwhelming bulk
of the U.N. membership — then (in the days before the overwhelming Afro-Asian influx into the U.N.) effectively everyone
but the Soviet Union and its immediate Eastern European
satellites. But the consequent United Nations inaction did
correspond, more or less, to the political reality of the immediate
post-war years until the time of Stalin's death in 1953, that no
action disturbing the immediate post-1945, *de facto* political-
military settlement in Europe could be taken unilaterally — that
is, by either the West on the one hand or the Soviet Union on the
other — without running the risk of escalation into full-scale
conflict. In this context, the law (meaning here, the Big-Power
Veto and the actual U.N. practice under it) simply followed the
social facts (meaning here, Bipolarity and the twin military bloc
system as the basic power configuration of post-war Europe and
of the post-war World generally).

The tacit acceptance, by both sides even during the height of
the Cold War era, of the constitutional law fact of the existence
of the Big-Power Veto, and also the propriety of its actual
exercise whenever a Big Power felt, however irrationally or
unfairly, that its own special interests were endangered or

threatened, explains the extreme fury with which Stalin and his political advisers greeted, in 1950, what they regarded as a unilateral, Western-promoted violation of the U.N. constitutional "rules of the game" over the Korean crisis.

On January 10th, 1950, the Soviet representative in the Security Council had submitted to the Security Council a draft resolution proposing that the Security Council should decide "not to recognise the credentials" of the representative of Nationalist China (then, as now, the Chinese government-in-exile in Taiwan after its military defeat and withdrawal from the mainland), "and to exclude him from the Security Council". After the rejection of this proposal, the Soviet representative walked out of the Security Council, and did not return to it until August 1st, 1950, when, under the ordinary Security Council system of regular rotation of its chairmanship, the Soviet representative, Mr. Malik, became eligible to be President of the Security Council. In the meantime, however, on June 25th, 1950, the Security Council, taking note of the invasion of South Korean territory by North Korean forces, adopted (in the absence of the Soviet representative) a resolution declaring that the North Korean action constituted a breach of the peace and calling for the withdrawal of the North Korean forces. On June 27th, 1950, the Security Council voted to recommend that members of the United Nations furnish assistance to the Republic of Korea; and on July 7th, 1950, the Security Council proceeded to established a unified military command, under the command of the United States.

When the Soviet representative, Mr. Malik, returned to the Security Council, in August, 1950, he bitterly denounced the action taken by the Security Council in the absence of the Soviet representative. To quote from the Security Council debates on the Korean issue, Mr. Malik charged:

> Taking advantage of the absence from the Security Council of . . . two permanent members — the USSR and China [Mr. Malik means, here, *Communist* China] — and dictating its will in the Council to its military and political allies, the United States has hurriedly forced upon the Council a series of illegal and indeed scandalous resolutions, designed on the one hand to cover up United States aggression in Korea and, on the other, to promote to the furthest possible extent the plans for war in Korea and the Far East by involving other States in this war. . . .

The resolutions adopted in the Security Council under the dictate of the United States delegation and in violation of the United Nations Charter have no legal force. They were motivated by the desire of the aggressor to cloak and mask his aggression and are in no way directed towards strengthening the cause of peace.

Even stronger invective was reserved by Soviet jurists for the famous "Uniting for Peace" Resolution, passed by the U.N. General Assembly on November 3rd, 1950, by a vote of 52 to 5, with 2 abstentions. This was the occasion when the U.N. General Assembly laid down the doctrine that the exercise of the veto by a Big-Power in the Security Council should not paralyse the U.N. or relieve the General Assembly of its power under the U.N. Charter. The Resolution — Resolution 377 A (V) — declares that:

... if the Security Council, because of lack of unanimity of the permanent members, fails to exercise its *primary* responsibility for maintenance of international peace and security in any case ... then the General Assembly shall consider the matter immediately with a view to making appropriate recommendations to Members for collective measures, including in the case of a breach of the peace or act of aggression the use of armed force when necessary, to maintain or restore international peace and security.

In terms of the "Uniting for Peace" Resolution, if the General Assembly is not in session when any such threat to the peace, breach of the peace, or act of aggression occurs, then it may meet in an emergency special session within 24 hours of a request therefor, initiated either by the Security Council on the vote of any seven members, or by a majority of members of the United Nations.

In the debate on the "Uniting for Peace" Resolution in the General Assembly, the chief Soviet delegate, the late Andrei Vyshinsky, saw the Resolution (correctly, I think, in terms of its intent) as designed to circumvent the Security Council and its special voting provisions allowing for the Big-Power Veto. Mr. Vyshinsky interpreted the effect of the resolution (again correctly, in my opinion) as being to attempt to revise the Charter principles dividing legal competence between the Security Council and the General Assembly, and thereby to weaken the Security Council in its special rôle as a guardian of Big-Power interests.

Looking back on the Korean crisis of 1950 and the legal measures taken in the United Nations to resolve that conflict in accordance with the Charter's principles, it is clear, in retrospect, that there was a certain element of *ad hoc*-ness in the Western tactical legal response. Just after the peaceful resolution of another, but later, Soviet-Western crisis — the Cuban missile crisis of October, 1962, — the then U.S. Assistant Secretary of State, Harlan Cleveland, gave some sage advice as to *methods* of problem-solving for Cold War conflicts:

> If we are to add one more 'lesson from flaps we have known' it would be this: Watch carefully the precedents you set. You will have to live with the institutions you create. The law you make may be your own.

The Security Council action in the Summer of 1950, taken in the absence of the Soviet Union after their earlier walk-out over the non-seating of Communist China, may have been militarily necessary to avert a North Korean take-over of South Korea. But it violated Soviet conceptions of parliamentary legality, for in Soviet legislative bodies an absence is considered equivalent to a negative vote; and it also disturbed a number of Western jurists, to judge by the debate in Western scientific legal journals, as to both its legality and also as to its political wisdom. I have no doubt that the chain of events whereby the Soviet Union continued to be absent during the crucial Security Council debates and votes on the U.N. Korean action resulted from a lack of adequate policy coordination and liaison between the U.N. operations division of the Soviet Foreign Ministry and Soviet military planners (something that occurs quite as often in the Soviet Union as in the West), rather than from any rooted Soviet conviction that the Soviet Union's absence *per se* would legally paralyse the Security Council. From the viewpoint of Western legal tacticians, the maximisation of the political-military advantages of Security Council-authorised action in Korea would have to be weighed against the resultant damage, if any, to the U.N. constitutional "rules of the game" as they were then known and observed by both sides in the Cold War struggle.

More serious from the viewpoint of the damage done to settled expectations as to conduct and method of operation of U.N. organs, however, is the "Uniting for Peace" Resolution. In the light of the military action already authorised and taken by the Security Council — albeit in the absence of the Soviet Union — to resolve the Korean crisis, it may be doubted whether the "Uniting for Peace" Resolution achieved any purpose other than to serve as an additional legal argument — *ex abundante cautela,* as it were — just in case the Western-based legal arguments, as to the non-equivalence of a Soviet absence from the Security Council to a Soviet veto in the Security Council, should fail to jell in the court of World public opinion.

This is why I mentioned Harlan Cleveland's sage advice as to the danger of having one's own *ad hoc* legal arguments boomerang, and be turned against one in the future. The Big-Power Veto in the Security Council is a political and legal protection for the Soviet Union, of course, but it can also be useful to the other Big-Powers. The Big-Power Veto, and in fact the general preponderance of the Security Council vis-à-vis the General Assembly, were designed as a recognition of the hard political reality of the post-1945 World, that the Big-Powers were the really "responsible" states on whom the ultimate burden of peace or war would rest. More than one Western jurist, in the last several years, responding to a conceived arbitrariness and capriciousness and immaturity — "irresponsibility", if you wish — of the U.N. General Assembly since the marked inflation in its numbers that occurred with the introduction of the flood of "new" countries from Asia, Africa, and the Caribbean, has had second thoughts about the "Uniting for Peace" Resolution and the merits of a policy of favouring — despite the historical intentions of the original drafters of the U.N. Charter — an accretion of political decision-making powers to the General Assembly at the expense of the Security Council. At the time the Uniting for Peace Resolution was adopted by the General Assembly — on November 3rd, 1950 — there was, as the near unanimous vote indicates, a substantial pro-Western, or Western-leaning, majority in the General Assembly. This, of course, is no longer true today. Whether, in the sort of Third French Republic political instability or voting anarchy that now prevails in the General Assembly, a more flexible Soviet political position, with more scope for flair and independent initiative in the manoeuvring in the General Assembly, might encourage the Soviet Union to reverse its earlier, "defensive era", pro-Security Council conservatism, in favour of trying to build a "revolutionary" coalition in the General Assembly under its own leadership and so to adopt erstwhile, Western, "all power to the General Assembly" legal-institutional positions, is another matter. What can be said, at least today, is that many Western jurists, looking at the actual record of the U.N. General Assembly performance, at the most recent 20th and 21st sessions in particular—at the all too frequent noisiness and playing to the gallery, on the part of many countries, and at the deplorable double standards, as between their own internal (frequently Police State) arbitrariness and the norms that these countries wish to apply to countries other than themselves—, have concluded that the quiet and sober business of international problem-solving is really too important to be entrusted to such an unstable and uncertain and unpredictable body; and that it might be wiser, instead, to return to the original, U.N. Founding Fathers', intent and to entrust the major issues of choice between Peace and War to the Big-Power dominated Security Council, or for that matter to direct, bilateral, Summit Meeting-type negotiation between the major powers.

Whatever the present-day potentialities for a Soviet flirtation, along politically adventurist lines of the nature outlined by the late Professor Korovin, with the new forces of political activism in the General Assembly, the old Soviet attitudes of caution and reserve vis-à-vis the General Assembly remain. Western students of Soviet international law notice a certain inevitable time lag—just as in our own, Western, society—between Soviet international legal doctrine on the one hand, and Soviet political self-interest and advantage as that might seem to be dictated in concrete cases. There is a terminal value, as Dewey has noted, in old legal ideas; and sometimes the doctrinal legal response to a present political problem is, in Soviet society as in our own, several years out of date in terms of political reality. Old legal ideas and dogma need constantly to be re-examined, in this regard, in terms of the extent to which they really continue to be useful in actual problem-solving. Suffice it to say that current Soviet international legal doctrinal writings are still pointed to a very major extent to the condemnation of alleged abuses of legal authority and powers on the part of an allegedly Western-dominated General Assembly.

Thus the Soviet Union has never taken kindly to the idea of U.N. Peace-Keeping operations, which have been one of the principal outlets for U.N.-based political activism over the decade or so since the Suez crisis of 1956. The legal argument advanced by the Soviet Union has been that, in terms of Article 43 of the U.N. Charter, the sole competence as to authorisation and establishment of U.N. armed forces is allocated to the Security Council where, of course, the Big-Power Veto operates. The first main political occasion for advancing this legal argument was in regard to the U.N. Middle East operation resulting from the combined British-French-Israeli attack on Egypt and the Suez Canal area in 1956; and there the Soviet Union's position has been that the acts on the basis of which the U.N. armed forces were set up lacked legal force since adopted by General Assembly resolution. It is in relation to the U.N. Congo operation, however, that the Soviet objections have been most vociferous since the U.N. operation clearly, in the end, redounded to the Soviet Union's political disadvantage. Since the Soviet Union had itself participated in the U.N. Security Council debate authorising the setting up of the U.N. Congo armed force and had in fact voted in support of the relevant Security Council resolution of July 14th, 1960 (which was approved by eight votes, with three abstentions: China, France, and the United Kingdom), it could not contest the legality of the actual setting up of the U.N. force. Instead, it had to concentrate its fire on the procedures actually used to form the force and its practical activities in the Congo. This the Soviet Union did, once it became clear that the U.N. force under U.N. Secretary General Dag Hammarskjöld's initiative — while it might be intended to prevent the re-establishment, with Belgian military support, of Belgian political and economic influence in the Congo in the person of the Katanga separatist leader, Moïse Tschombé — certainly would not be used to establish Soviet political influence in its place, in the person of breakaway, leftist-leaning Premier, Patrice Lumumba. The Soviet Union had reversed its earlier hard-and-fast opposition to international armed forces of whatever nature, and had voted in the Security

Council in favour of the U.N. Congo force, in the first place, mainly because the anarchy and virtually complete absence of governmental authority that succeeded on the proclamation of independence for the Congo on June 30th, 1960, had set the stage for a Belgian return and provoked the anguished joint appeal for help to the U.N. made by Premier Lumumba and President Kasavubu. Here it was one case, then, where the emotional "anti-Colonialist" cluster of international legal values successfully outweighed, in Soviet thinking, the more cautious, prosaic, "institutional" cluster of international legal values with their clear preference for confining jurisdictional competence to authorise U.N. activism to the Security Council where the Big-Power Veto could operate as a defence of Soviet vital interests if need be.

Once disillusioned over the non-fulfilment of its original high hopes as to the outcome of the U.N. action in the Congo, the Soviet Union could not afford to forget or to forgive. The Soviet Union never pardoned Dag Hammarskjöld for his opting in favour of President Kasavubu and his supporters as the politically most stable and reliable group for building a viable, central government in the Congo. And so it undertook its personal vendetta against the U.N. Secretary-General aimed at preventing any further extension of his term of office, and ultimately at securing his replacement by a *troika* system of administration that would have seen the U.N. administration governed by a three-man board, representative, respectively, of the West, the Soviet bloc, and the neutralist "Third World", and that would, surely, have ended the U.N. organisation's rôle altogether as an independent political decision-making body.

The Soviet Union, likewise, refused to pay its U.N. General Assembly-assessed share of the U.N. peace-keeping operations, in the Congo and in the Middle East, contending in particular that the whole U.N. Congo operation, as actually conducted, was illegal. This led directly, following on the handing down of the World Court Advisory Opinion on Certain Expenses of the United Nations, to the United States-sponsored show-down, in the U.N. General Assembly at its 19th session in the Fall of 1964, over the Soviet and French non-payment of the special financial assessments resulting from the U.N. Congo and Middle East operations. The United States attempt, then, to apply Article 19 of the U.N. Charter and to take away the Soviet and French votes in the General Assembly so long as the special dues remained unpaid, brought the work of the General Assembly to a complete standstill for the 19th session; until the United States finally backed down, against a threatened break-up of the U.N. organisation altogether, and allowed the work of the succeeding 20th session of the General Assembly to proceed without resolving the U.N. Expenses issue. The Soviet Union and France, to this day, have so far failed to pay the special assessments, and have resisted various face-saving formulae and devices designed to allow them to back down gracefully if they should wish to retreat.

Beyond this, the Soviet Union maintains an unyielding opposition to any suggestion of a stand-by U.N. military force or an international police force in any form — as being designed merely to utilise the United Nations for "Colonialist" ends. In the same issue of a recent Soviet scientific legal publication that characterises the present writer as one of "colonialism's theoreticians", Canadian Prime Minister Lester B. Pearson is castigated for his support of the principle of an international police force. In the Soviet journal's words:

> Canada's Prime Minister Pearson proposes a stand-by peace force, 'formally outside the United Nations but ready to be used at its request', 'for preserving the peace; for carrying out and supervising U.N. recommendations when called on; for pacifying disturbed areas; and for putting the international police force behind international decisions'. In other words, a new form of police operations by the imperialists is suggested, while 'pacifying disturbed areas' apparently means suppression of the national-liberation movement.

It is this form of intransigent Soviet opposition, born of an original Soviet legal doctrinal position, and buttressed by bitter Soviet practical experience in the concrete case of the Congo, that renders further progress in the direction of establishing any U.N. emergency force extremely difficult, and thus renders essential the examination and study of alternative methods of U.N.-based peace-keeping.

THE U.N. CHARTER: **IV**
TREATY OR CONSTITUTION?

The Changing Rôle of the World Court

In his dissenting judicial opinion on Certain Expenses of the
United Nations — the Advisory Opinion handed down by the
World Court on July 20th, 1962, whose majority position pre-
cipitated the Western-sponsored action, in terms of Article 19 of
the U.N. Charter, to deprive the Soviet Union and France of
their vote in the U.N. General Assembly — the then President of
the Court, the Polish jurist, Judge Winiarski, formulated principles of interpretation which reveal, very dramatically, basic
legal doctrinal differences between Soviet bloc and Western
jurists as to the nature and character of the Charter. As President
Winiarski commented:

> The Charter, a multilateral treaty which was the result of prolonged and
> laborious negotiations, carefully created organs and determined their
> competence and means of action.

> The intention of those who drafted it was clearly to abandon the possi-
> bility of useful action rather than to sacrifice the balance of carefully estab-
> lished fields of competence, as can be seen, for example, in the case of
> voting in the Security Council. It is only by such procedures, which were
> clearly defined, that the United Nations can seek to achieve its purposes.
> It may be that the United Nations is sometimes not in a position to under-
> take action which would be useful for the maintenance of international
> peace and security or for one or another of the purposes indicated in
> Article 1 of the Charter, but that is the way in which the Organisation was
> conceived and brought into being . . . .

Judge Koretsky of the Soviet Union made this same point, but
even more succinctly, in his own dissenting opinion in the same
case:

I am prepared to stress the necessity of the strict observation and proper interpretation of the provisions of the Charter, its rules, without limiting itself by reference to the purposes of the Organisation: otherwise one would have to come to the long ago condemned formula: 'The ends justify the means.'

Now, since the majority of the World Court, in the Advisory Opinion on U.N. Expenses, upheld the validity of the expenditures authorised by the General Assembly in behalf of the U.N. military operations in the Middle East and in the Congo, as being legitimate "expenses of the Organisation" within the meaning of Article 17(2) of the Charter, it would be tempting to try, in political realist terms, to explain, if not to write off altogether, the two Soviet bloc judges' dissenting opinions as being purely *ad hoc* judicial responses to the political self-interest of the individual judges' parent countries. Such a nakedly cynical interpretation, however, would ignore two very important considerations. First, the two Soviet bloc judges are not ranged as lone dissenters against the rest of the World Court in the U.N. Expenses reference: it is, after all, a 9-to-5 holding, with the two Soviet bloc judges being joined, in dissent, by the French judge, Judge Basdevant (which fact, of course, might also lend itself to "political realist"–type interpretations of the judicial vote), but also by the two Latin American, Civil Law, jurists, Judge Moreno Quintana and Judge Bustamante y Rivero, who under no circumstances could be accused of secretly favouring the Soviet bloc and French political positions on the legality of the General Assembly's special financial assessments for the Middle East and Congo operations.

Second, and beyond this, however, there is a long and detailed history of Soviet, and Soviet bloc, doctrinal writing, since the establishment of the United Nations Organisation in 1945, which directly accords with President Winiarski and Judge Koretsky's intellectual position in the U.N. Expenses reference, and from which, indeed, their opinions may be said directly to flow. Summarised briefly, this long-term Soviet doctrinal legal position, vis-à-vis the United Nations, has been that the U.N. Charter is merely a treaty — a multilateral treaty at that — which for certain limited purposes may operate to restrict the national sovereignty of its individual national signatories; but that, like all treaties or other international arrangements purporting to restrict national sovereignty, it is to be strictly construed and in any case against those arguing for the restriction of national sovereignty. Such an intellectual position as to modes of interpretation of the Charter corresponds to those intellectual legal attitudes found in the English-speaking, Common Law countries which insist that statutes, and particularly those derogating from the civil liberties of the private citizen, are to be strictly construed and in any case against the claimed derogation from the private citizen's rights. It is reflected, again, in President Winiarski's further comments, in the U.N. Expenses reference — in reply to the legal argument that the course of actual practice, at the General Assembly over the years, warranted the World Court's accepting a new legal gloss as having been effectively created upon the Charter in supplement to the bare bones of its actual text:

> Reliance has been placed upon practice as providing justification for an affirmative answer to the question submitted to the Court. The technical budgetary practice of the Organisation has no bearing upon the question, which is a question of law . . . .

> It is . . . difficult to assert, in the case before the Court, either that practice can furnish a canon of construction warranting an affirmative answer to the question addressed to the Court, or that it may have contributed to the establishment of a legal rule particular to the Organisation, created *praeter legem*, and, still less, that it can have done so *contra legem*.

The countervailing intellectual legal approach to that evidenced by President Winiarski and Judge Koretsky, and their colleagues in dissent in the U.N. Expenses reference, is that favoured by a number of Western jurists, and summed up, in terms of distinctive Western municipal law attitudes, in the celebrated dictum of the great Chief Justice John Marshall of the United States Supreme Court: "Never forget that it is a constitution that we are expounding!" The essence of this particular approach is to be found in the conception that law is not a frozen cake of doctrine whose meaning jelled once and for all in some bygone age; but that it is, instead, a continuing process of creative adjustment of old rules and principles to rapidly changing societal interests and expectations. The importance of the statute/constitution dichotomy lies in the fact that while, with an ordinary statute which is presumably capable of fairly easy amendment by direct legislative action, it may be reasonable to expect the interests in certainty, and in stability and predictability of settled expectations, to rank very highly, this is not the case with a constitution which, by definition, is intended to endure through the ages without too many formal changes, and which therefore needs a very wide amplitude of construction and interpretation if it is to be accommodated to radically new societal problems.

Those who prefer to view the U.N. Charter as a constitution, and not a mere statute, insist that it must constantly be re-examined in the light of its original grand design as an instrument for maintaining World peace; and that the bald text of the Charter must therefore be supplemented, and strict-and-literal interpretation eschewed, in favour of policy interpretations that will shape and refine and re-state the details so as to accord to these ultimate historical purposes and objectives.

In retrospect, neither the Soviet nor the Western policy preferences, as between these two radically different approaches to the Charter yielding in the long run radically different sorts of answers to the basic type of problem-solving that the United Nations has been concerned with since its formation in 1945, is really very surprising. For each choice, Soviet and Western, is an example of instrumental legal thinking. In the case of the Soviet Union, strict and literal interpretation as a methodological approach to construction of the Charter was especially attuned to the sort of defensive, holding operation, type of tactics that the Soviet Union felt to be enjoined for itself in an era when the Soviet Union and its political associates represented a tiny minority who were consistently and repeatedly outvoted by hostile Western-dominated coalitions in the U.N. policy-making organs. In the case of the major Western countries, since, right from the outset of the United Nations, they seemed to have comfortable pro-Western voting majorities in all main policy-making organs, they could confidently indulge in broad, policy-making, legislative, approaches to the U.N. Charter, secure in the knowledge that any creative re-writing or re-definition of the Charter's provisions, or any new gloss created upon its text, would, at the very least, not be inimical to Western vital interests. It is in this sense that some prominent Western jurists vigorously championed the legality of the U.N. Security Council action in the Summer of 1950, in the Korean crisis, in the absence of the Soviet representative, and also the General Assembly's Uniting for Peace Resolution adopted shortly thereafter — as examples of creative re-interpretation of the U.N. Charter in the full spirit of its original historical purposes; just as Soviet jurists challenged the very same Security Council and General Assembly actions as unwarranted departures from the strict provisions of the Charter and gross violations, therefore, of international law. And we saw the same essential differences of opinion, as between Western and Soviet jurists, over the U.N. Expenses issue.

The point is, of course, that an intellectual dichotomy of this sort — between purposive, policy-oriented, interpretation on the one hand, and strict-and-literal interpretation on the other — is as common in our own national, constitutional law, as in international law. Policy-oriented interpretations are, perhaps, more palatable in internal, municipal law, because there will normally be present, there, a sufficient general societal consensus to approve and ratify the constitutional re-writing or novation that in fact is being invoked, in the name of a "policy interpretation", to adjust old positive law to new societal conditions. Such a general societal consensus hardly exists, however, to the same necessary minimum degree, in a World Community characterised by political-military Bipolarity and Ideological conflict in general. It therefore behoves us to be modest in attempting to force through startling new changes in the pre-existing Cold War "ground rules", in the name of a "policy interpretation" of the Charter. There is merit in the current Soviet juristic criticism of the inherent subjectivity of some of the main Western approaches to interpretation of the Charter. As a younger Soviet jurist, writing in the most recent issue of the Soviet Yearbook, declares:

> The main arguments of the Western jurists are based on the theory of the so-called inherent capacity, 'implied powers' and the 'principle of efficacy'. The advocates of this theory justify any breach of the Charter by counterposing the articles which define the purposes and principles of the Organisation to articles which lay down the procedure of activity and

delimit the competence of organs designated for achieving these purposes. The latter, in the opinion of bourgeois jurists, can be overlooked because they supposedly are of a purely technical, procedural nature.

•   •   •

Distinctive national attitudes as to the U.N. Charter, and in particular, as to whether it should be viewed as a mere statute (treaty) to be restrictively interpreted, or instead as a constituton, have tended, in the years since establishment of the United Nations in 1945, to be paralleled by distinctive national attitudes to the World Court, and to its jurisdiction and special competence, in a World Community in process of rapid and fundamental change. In our own internal, municipal law there are two main competing conceptions as to the proper rôle and functions of a constitutional court. One view is that a Supreme Court has a purely limited, dependent position in the general constitutional structure; that it should construe its rôle narrowly, and exercise self-restraint, and thus immunise itself as much as possible from great political *causes célèbres*. The other view is that, where there exist practical break-downs or obstructions, in the exercise of their normal rôles, on the part of the main, executive and legislative, organs of community policy-making, the judges should move in boldly to fill the gap and to legislate, in effect, interstitially: here we have judicially-based activism in the cause of effective community policy-making.

Now both these conceptions of the judicial function — judicial self-restraint and judicial activism — are to be found on the part of international lawyers in regard to the World Court, in the early, post–World War II years. Soviet jurists, responding to the obvious political fact of the Soviet bloc judges being a tiny minority in an essentially Western law-derived, or Western law-influenced, tribunal, tended to argue the merits of judicial self-restraint and of the World Court's avoiding any overt policy-making, legislating, activist rôle. Western jurists, in spite of a certain governmental timorousness as to submitting to the compulsory jurisdiction of the Court — this a response, normally, to internal, neo-isolationist forces in their own countries, as with the so-called Connally Amendment reservation to the United States' adherence to the Court's jurisdiction — have tended to be far more confident and enthusiastic about the affirmative possibilities for the Court's essaying a law-making, legislative, rôle.

In the most recent decision announced by the World Court, however — in July, 1966, on the complaint by Ethiopia and Liberia against the Union of South Africa, in respect to the South-West Africa Mandate — , these intellectual attitudes had become strangely blurred and scrambled, in response, in measure, to the vast changes in the United Nations as a whole and in particular in the General Assembly, as a result of the admission in the past few years of the flood of "new", Afro-Asian countries. The actual disappearance of the Western, or Western-leaning, majority in the General Assembly, and the further presaging of widespread changes in the make-up and composition of the World Court itself as the new forces in the General Assembly learn to marshal their voting strength effectively, are reflected in measure in the crossing of erstwhile intellectual lines in the World Court, in the South-West Africa case judgment.

The actual decision of the World Court in the South-West Africa case was achieved by a bare majority of one, after the President, the Australian judge, Sir Percy Spender, had exercised his right to cast a second, tie-breaking vote, when the Court had first deadlocked seven-seven (including Sir Percy's first vote, as an ordinary member of the Court). The decision of the World Court, it must be said, has ample precedent in the domestic jurisprudence of most legal systems, whether Common Law or Civil Law. Courts do have the right to avoid ruling on substantive legal issues, by deciding on narrow procedural points: judicial self-restraint is a recognised legal virtue in many countries, both Western and Communist, especially, one might say, where great political *causes célèbres* are involved. Again, on the record of their individual performances, both as judges on the World Court and also, more importantly perhaps, in their pre-Court careers, there is nothing that warrants partisan interpretation that the individual judges in the World Court majority gave a purely *ad hoc*, arbitrary, personal political response to the substantive policy issue involved in the South-West Africa case. In the case of the President, Sir Percy Spender, his intellectual position in the South-West Africa case accords with the general legal thinking of a leader of the Equity bar, which Sir Percy at

44

one time was; and also with the special legal philosophy of judicial self-restraint and of the practical political limits to the rôle of a Supreme Court judge, developed by the late Mr. Justice Felix Frankfurter of the United States Supreme Court who strongly influenced Sir Percy Spender in his general legal ideas when he was Australian Ambassador to the United States in the years immediately prior to his election to the World Court in 1957.

It is especially worth noting, in the South-West Africa judgment, that the Polish member of the World Court, Judge Winiarski, chose to part company with the Soviet member, Judge Koretsky, and himself join Sir Percy Spender in helping to make the court majority. In Judge Winiarski's case, the more basic Soviet bloc legal position as to the general un-wisdom of the World Court's indulging in any policy-making, legislating, "political" rôle in an era of ideological divisions in the World Community prevailed, over any immediate temptations to establish a special exception to general Soviet bloc legal doctrine and to cast a triumphantly "anti-Colonialist" vote in the South-West Africa case.

Nevertheless, it must be said that, in the manner and form in which the World Court decision was rendered in the South-West Africa case, it must be considered to be something in the nature of a disaster for the general cause of World Law. For the actual, narrow procedural point on which the World Court majority managed to decide the South-West Africa case, thereby avoiding ruling on the substantive legal issues — including the burning issue of the compatibility of the Union of South Africa government's *Apartheid* programme with International Law — would baffle the intellectual ingenuity even of the mediaeval schoolmen.

This narrow procedural point, accepted by the World Court majority in the South-West Africa case, was that while the complainants, Ethiopia and Liberia, did have legal standing to *bring* the suit — this had been upheld, in 1962, by a fifteen-man World Court, by an eight-to-seven vote, with Sir Percy Spender dissenting — the two complainant African States did not have legal standing to obtain a *decision* in the matter. It is not too much to say that if the fifteenth member of the World Court, Judge

Badawi of the United Arab Republic, had not died suddenly in 1965 (he had still not been replaced at the time of the final decision of the World Court in July 1966), the seven-seven tie of 1966 that was broken, against the complainant African States, by Sir Percy Spender's second, tie-breaking vote, would have been eight-to-seven in favour of the complainants.

The angry charges made by certain African delegates to the United Nations, after the announcement of the South-West Africa decision, that the World Court is a "white man's" court, and that the emergent countries can not expect their rights to be vindicated by *legal* action that involves recourse to a "white man's" international law, were not new. They were heard in the speeches of Afro-Asian delegates, in the past several years, in the United Nations Special Committee on Friendly Relations (Coexistence). What was new now, perhaps, was the vehemence and uninhibitedness of the comments being directed against the World Court and its members, and also the clamant character of the demands for direct, political action, instead of recourse to legal machinery.

Would the World Court have been better advised to delay decision still further — the matter had been before it for six years, after all, at the time that it actually handed down its decision in July, 1966; and the court itself is the sole judge of the timing and staging of its decisions? Like the *Dred Scott* decision of the United States Supreme Court, which hastened the onset of the American Civil War, the World Court might be said to have given a legally correct, but politically unwise, even irresponsible, decision, which other people, as well as the Court itself, would have to live with. For one immediate consequence of the decision, anticipated by certain foreign ministries, was to jeopardise prospects for ensuring that only jurists of genuine intellectual calibre and professional integrity would be nominated to, and elected to, the Court in the future: the periodical elections to the Court have always been somewhat cynical and horse-trading in character, even on the part of those major Western nations that officially are most committed to support of the Court and to extension of its jurisdiction. But the elections to the World Court in the Fall of 1966, immediately following on the South-West Africa decision, in spite of some genuinely outstanding choices like the near unanimous selection of the distinguished Polish jurist, Dr. Manfred Lachs, in succession to Judge Winiarski, tended to outdo all preceding United Nations' elections to the World Court, in political power plays that were attempted and brought off. History may well record that the American member of the Court, Judge Philip Jessup, more correctly sensed the "winds of change" in Africa and the general movement of World history when, in his dissenting opinion in the South-West Africa case, he refused to evade the substantive issue of the legality or otherwise of governmentally-practised racial differentiation or discrimination, at international law. In categorising the World Court majority position as "completely unfounded in law", Judge Jessup insisted that international law should not be treated as an outdated collection of dead rules, from some bygone era of World history; but that it "must take account of the views and attitudes of the contemporary international community". On this approach, Judge Jessup concluded: "The accumulation of expressions of condemnation of *Apartheid* are proof of the pertinent contemporary international standard."

. . .

In the end, the remedy of the "new", Afro-Asian countries for the political impasse created by the World Court's denial of jurisdiction as to the substantive issue in the South-West Africa case, was, after all, direct political action in the General Assembly, where the "new" countries' voting strength could best be utilised. By a vote of 114 to 2 (with three abstentions), the U.N. General Assembly voted, in late October, 1966, to declare the Union of South Africa's original, League of Nations–derived mandate to administer South-West Africa "terminated", and to declare that the territory now comes under "the direct responsibility" of the United Nations. These are bold words, of course, and how much they mean in fact will depend on the practical measures taken to give effect to them. While the African states, in general, were disposed to try to establish immediately a U.N. Administering Authority for South-West Africa, the Latin American nations moved successfully to substitute a fourteen-member, *ad hoc* committee to recommend, by April, 1967, "practical means" for U.N. administration of the territory.

At the same time, the Security Council voted, in December, 1966, to impose mandatory, but selective, economic sanctions against the breakaway white minority government of Rhodesia, to compel its acceptance of the principle of majority rule. This action fell far short of the comprehensive measures demanded by the African states in the United Nations, which included demands for the use of military force by Britain. But the action voted by the Security Council went as far as the British government itself felt politically prepared to go; and since the United States concluded that it had no reasonable alternative to supporting the British government's position, this was as much as the Security Council could agree upon.

This, plus another General Assembly resolution repeating a General Assembly vote at the Fall of 1965 session of the U.N., holding that the removal of military bases from non-self-governing territories is not an "important question" that requires a two-thirds majority in the General Assembly, in terms of Article 18(2) of the Charter, showed quite clearly that the two parliamentary organs of the U.N. — the Security Council and the General Assembly — have now become major arenas for the new political activism in the cause of "anti-Colonialism" generally. The vote of the General Assembly that a simple majority in the General Assembly is heretofore enough to adopt a resolution calling for the removal of military bases from non-self-governing territories, had originally been carried, at the 1965 session, by 59 to 45 with a large number of Asian and African states supporting the Soviet bloc countries on the issue. This was one of the principal bases for angry Western charges — by U.S. Ambassador to the United Nations, Arthur Goldberg, among others, after the 1965 session — that the "new", Afro-Asian countries had acted "irresponsibly" in thus suddenly and arbitrarily changing the "ground rules" as to an essential part of United Nations procedure. The repetition of this vote at the 1966 session, in spite of Western contentions that it was unconstitutional and therefore, in point of law, a complete nullity, was an indication both of a seeming African intent, with Asian and Soviet support, to ram through a record number of General Assembly resolutions demanding bold action without regard to the possibility of their practical enforcement; and also of the fact that the Soviet bloc may be prepared now to overcome the old Soviet, institutionally-based, scruples and reservations as to the legal competence of the General Assembly, in order to act as the residuary legatee of African anger at the political remnants of "colonialism".

.   .   .

Security Council measures, where they are not killed by the Big-Power Veto, are of course clearly international law, whatever their practical chances of success, in action, may be. What is the *legal* effect of U.N. General Assembly resolutions, now that the "new" countries are disposed to use their voting strength there to try to achieve direct political action? Many Western lawyers in recent years, having second thoughts about the political wisdom of the General Assembly's Uniting for Peace Resolution of 1950, are inclined now to deny the force of law to General Assembly resolutions. For *Soviet bloc*, as distinct from *Soviet* jurists, General Assembly resolutions reflect the "developing juridical conscience of people", which they see as acting on governments and thus creating international law norms. Dr. Vratislav Pechota, the brilliant younger Czech jurist, cites as examples of such "juridical conscience" effectuating itself in the creation of norms of international law, the "principle of general disarmament" and the "principle of the final liquidation of colonialism", both of which he sees as developed through successive General Assembly resolutions. Dr. Pechota differentiates between what he styles as "simple recommendations" on the one hand, and "solemn declarations" on the other, of the General Assembly, contending that it is the latter that act upon the practice of states and thereby engender either new norms, or else change old norms, of customary international law.

Professor Manfred Lachs, the Polish jurist, echoing these same thoughts, speaks of General Assembly resolutions in the area of self-determination of states, international trade exchanges, and also general disarmament, as leading to the formulation of "concrete and imperative principles" of international law. Answering some Western critics, Professor Lachs used pointedly to ask on what juridical base they regarded the legal efficacy of the principle of the non-orbiting of nuclear weapons in space vehicles, as being rested. Both the Soviet Union and the United States clearly regarded the principle as being mutually binding on each of them, from the time of its expression in a U.N. General Assembly resolution of October 17th, 1963. Yet where did its legal force come from, if it did not come from the General Assembly resolution? Of course, the principle is now being concretised in the new Treaty on the Peaceful Uses of Outer Space, whose actual text was agreed upon and finalised by the Soviet Union and the United States in December, 1966. But that, I am sure Professor Lachs would say, was done simply *ex abundante cautela*, and was in no way necessary to the validity of a principle that had already been law for three years or more.

Perhaps the most interesting answer to this particular legal problem — which is important because of the key it provides to more general, long-range attitudes taken by particular countries to the different U.N. organs, and also to the U.N. as a whole, as arenas for the effectuation and achievement of their own distinctive national policies — is to be found in contemporary Soviet legal doctrine. Professor Gregory Tunkin, the then Principal Legal Adviser to the Soviet Foreign Ministry, used to accord a certain deference to United Nations General Assembly resolutions; but unlike his Soviet bloc, Eastern European colleagues, he tended to view them, more cautiously, as only "subsidiary", auxiliary sources of international law. Two of the most recent Soviet juristic utterances on this point command special attention, however. Dr. Morozov suggests that General Assembly resolutions are a source of international law when adopted by states of the two socio-economic systems (Communist and Capitalist) and of all three main political groups (Socialist, Western, and Neutralist). Dr. Yanovsky agrees with this, but with the added proviso that the General Assembly resolutions, being agreed to by all three main political groups (Socialist, Western, and Neutralist), should also be adopted without dissenting vote.

I think these latest Soviet juristic statements are important for two reasons. First, they reaffirm the more cautious Soviet doctrinal legal positions which would allow the Soviet government, if need be in the future, to retreat politically and thus to refuse to recognise "irresponsible" General Assembly resolutions as having any legal effect. Second, they proclaim a legal principle, that itself comes very close to reflecting the essential political facts of life, and of effective power, in the contemporary World Community: that any international law norms that wish to lay claim to being viable must proceed from a genuine inter-systems consensus. In place of the old positivistic, law-as-command, theories, therefore, we now have explicit recognition by Soviet jurists of a new law-as-consensus approach, in which the emphasis must be upon bilateralism, and on mutuality and reciprocity of interest, as the basis of international law norm-making in a pluralist World Community.

*Nuclear and General Disarmament
in an Era of Ideological Conflict*

It is apparent, by now, that while Disarmament, and particularly Nuclear Disarmament, has sometimes been viewed in the past as a sort of universal panacea for the assorted ills of the World Community, it cannot really be usefully separated, as a legal principle, from other, more or less peremptory principles of contemporary international law — what the Soviet Union, for purposes of its own sponsored East-West dialogue, has called the International Law of Peaceful Coexistence, and what the United Nations has preferred to label, instead, as the Principles of Friendly Relations and Cooperation among States. The failure, in particular, practically to implement the principle that states shall settle their international disputes by peaceful means — through the inability so far to devise, and financially to sustain, effective permanent, institutionally-based peace-keeping procedures, because of the Soviet-Western conflict over the respective rôles of the U.N. General Assembly and the Security Council; and the further failure to concretise the principle that states refrain from the threat or use of force against the territorial integrity or political independence of any state — through the inability, so far, to agree on a workable legal definition of "aggression" — all mean that the contribution of jurists (whether in the United Nations and its specialised agencies or elsewhere), in terms of the elaboration and refinement of legal principles of Disarmament, can only be a dependent or relative one to the overall task of securing the renunciation of war as an instrument for effectuating national policy.

It is also apparent, at the more strictly political level, that substantial progress in the direction of general or complete Disarmament is dependent upon and conditioned by progress in other and related political fields—for example, in that difficult area of policy concerned with the balancing, on the one hand, of undoubted interests in security and stability of settled expectations as to existing territorial frontiers, and, on the other hand, interests in self-determination of peoples and in the satisfaction of claims of ethnic-cultural minorities that may have been allocated to one national control or another, more or less arbitrarily, through the political accidents of the post–World War II peace settlements and military occupations.

Premier Khrushchev's celebrated New Year's Eve message issued on December 31st, 1963, and sent to all Heads of States, which called for the renunciation of force in territorial disputes, represents one view of this particular problem. Western responses to the Khrushchev missive were, on the whole, rather cautious and even reserved, reacting no doubt to a certain cloudiness and imprecision of language in the Khrushchev message, which Western statesmen—understandably, perhaps, in view of certain Soviet official positions and statements on these issues in the past—may have felt to be contrived and deliberate, so as to allow the Soviet Union certain built-in escape clauses from any general renunciation of force in territorial disputes, in terms of exceptions like "wars of liberation", infiltration by "volunteers", and the like. The concept of "wars of liberation", in particular, is one which, from their actual record of experience in concrete dealings with the Soviet Union, Western statesmen and jurists have frequently considered to be largely self-defining from the Soviet viewpoint.

Yet, in retrospect—and this serves as a commentary on the standards of international fact-finding and of the general state of intelligence services, and information, on each side as to the other side's intentions, during the Cold War era—it really does seem that Premier Khrushchev may have meant just what he said when he called for the renunciation of force in *territorial* disputes. For the Soviet Union today, far more perhaps than at any earlier period in its history, since the October revolution of 1917, has a very substantial interest and stake in the sanctity of territorial boundaries, and in their preservation against other than peaceful, consensual change. Certainly, the strongest support for present-day Soviet territorial boundaries, whether in post-war Europe, or else in Asia, where the nineteenth-century Tsarist territorial expansionism is already being actively and publicly disputed today by Communist China, lies in traditional or classical international law doctrine, preferably not too flexibly or imaginatively applied or reinterpreted in present-day terms. Old territorial treaties or agreements, originally assisted by military occupation or the presence of superior military power generally, are to be governed today by the principle of *pacta sunt servanda* — strict observance — without too many latter-day second thoughts as to radical international law innovations like the Soviet-developed special exception of "unequal treaties". "Unequal treaties" — meaning treaties where there was a gross disproportionality in bargaining power as between the two sides — are, by definition, not binding at law: the Soviet Union developed this special legal concept to free itself from the Treaty of Brest-Litovsk, made by Lenin with Imperial Germany in 1917 to take Russia out of World War I, and from other onerous Treaty obligations that redounded to Russia's disadvantage and that dated either from Tsarist days or else from the immediate, post-1917, Revolutionary Years when the Soviet's power was weak: the Soviet Union, however, for all practical purposes, seems to regard the concept of "unequal treaties" as being dead today, and in any case as not available for legal use against itself in any contemporary problem-situation.

Likewise, the Western-favoured international legal doctrine, as to treaties, of *clausula rebus sic stantibus* — meaning, here, the necessity for treaties being conditioned, in their practical interpretation and application, today, by regard to the background political, social, and economic facts against which they were signed and the changes in those same facts today — is viewed by Soviet jurists with disdain or sometimes outright hostility. Simple *occupatio*, in relation to territorial claims, on this view, derives strength from long-time use and control, uncluttered by contemporary heretical notions as to self-determination or the necessity for consent of the original local, indigenous populations: the principle of self-determination tends to be reserved by Soviet jurists as a privilege of "colonial" peoples, whom Soviet jurists seem to define restrictively, with an exclusively anti-Western orientation.

The conclusion that Premier Khrushchev's New Year's Eve message, of December 31st, 1963, was in reality far more serious and substantial in Soviet eyes than any casually mischievous ploy at embarrassing and confusing the West in an area where the West (taking note of the substantial Overseas, "colonial" holdings — past, and in some cases, also, present — of a number of members of NATO and the Western military alliance system generally) has been traditionally at a profound psychological, and also practical political, disadvantage, is strengthened by recourse to Soviet scientific legal writing, both before and after Premier Khrushchev's message. What these scientific legal writings reveal is a sustained Soviet intellectual campaign to legitimate both the present Soviet territorial frontiers and also the *de facto* political-military frontiers of 1945 in Central Europe. There is also a substantial and carefully designed attempt to anticipate, and to defeat in advance, any Chinese Communist attempts at revision of existing Sino-Soviet territorial boundaries, based on a Soviet-style "unequal treaties" argument; for part of the Soviet drive, in the scientific legal literature, is to enumerate, with great public pride, asserted historical examples of renunciation by the Soviet Union, of its own free will and at its own initiative, of treaties from the era of Tsarist Russia that violated the rights of peoples in Asian countries — the clear implication being that any and all such treaties have long since been denounced by the Soviet Union.

The conclusion seems clear that Premier Khrushchev's New Year's Eve, December 31st, 1963, message was a Soviet defensive, or if you wish, anticipatory, move directed against Communist China; and that Western political leaders, due to failure of their advisers on Soviet affairs correctly to read the signals, missed the point entirely and construed the Soviet leader's ploy as being simply a continuation of old line, Soviet-Western, Cold War manoeuvring for political advantage. As a result of this, and also of that certain timorousness or unimaginativeness observable on the part of Western policy-makers in the immediate aftermath of President Kennedy's death, a certain opportunity seems to have been lost of legally consolidating with the Soviet Union, on a reciprocal, formal basis, that quite considerable investment, in stability of settled expectations and in historical continuity in the legal development and effectuation of social change that customary international law, properly applied, is supposed to effectuate and assist.

.   .   .

The principle of self-determination of peoples is postulated as one of the primary principles of Friendly Relations (Coexistence), without any guide-lines being offered as to its relation (whether hierarchically superior or subordinate) to the other postulated principles of Friendly Relations such as, in particular, the principle of prohibition of the threat or use of force, and the principle of peaceful settlement of disputes. It seems clear, however, that any really comprehensive scheme of Disarmament, in the future, between the Soviet bloc and the West, can hardly avoid being related to the finality or otherwise of the general post-war political settlement in Middle-Europe, especially the problem of Berlin and the two Germanies. While particular proposals for solution here — such as the idea of a non-aggression pact between NATO and the Warsaw Pact organisation (which was mooted, once more, in President Johnson's special White House Conference on International Cooperation, in late 1965) — may be faulted one way or another as being perhaps purely *ad hoc*, and necessarily limited, responses to a more long-range and far more complex political problem, they do at least recognise the interdependence of all main international legal problems of the present day, and the desirability, and indeed inevitability, of attempting some substantial reduction of political tensions in Europe if a real breakthrough is to be made in achieving Soviet-Western accord over Disarmament.

The most significant achievement of recent years, indeed of the whole post-war era, in the area of Disarmament, was a direct product of the general Soviet-Western *détente* that so closely followed on the peaceful resolution of the Soviet-Western confrontation of October, 1962, over the Cuban missile crisis. This, of course, was the Moscow Partial Test Ban Treaty of August, 1963; and it was itself closely followed by the further accord, that was expressed in the U.N. General Assembly Resolution of October 17, 1963, on the non-orbiting of nuclear weapons in space vehicles, now finally recorded in treaty form in the new Treaty on the Peaceful Uses of Outer Space. It must be acknowledged that the societal facts in the World Community have changed markedly since the time that the Moscow Test Ban Treaty was achieved in 1963 — most notably in terms of the key participants in the World power process. While it is true that neither Communist China — nor, for that matter, France — adhered to the Moscow Partial Test Ban Treaty of 1963, in spite of the well-nigh universality of its acceptance, Communist Chinese non-participation was obviously far less significant in the period before Communist China had exploded her first nuclear devices and thus forced her way into the "nuclear club". The question today is whether, in the light of Communist China's actual and potential nuclear capability, with the probability that she will soon develop operationally workable nuclear delivery systems, any really effective international law principles, as to Nuclear Disarmament in particular, can be worked out and be expected to be applied in the World Community, without Communist Chinese adherence and also participation in actually framing them. On the other hand, in the face of Communist China's continued non-representation in the United Nations, and her current apparent intransigence in regard to the possibility of joining in the future, is it worthwhile inviting Communist China to take part in the World nuclear disarmament dialogue? This is clearly the principal dilemma of political choice as to Disarmament, of the present time. For it involves balancing, on the one hand, the very real possibility of some *smaller* consensus as to Disarmament that would necessarily be limited as to the countries taking part in it, but that would at least involve countries sharing certain minimum principles of World Public Order, if not, as yet, common legal values in general; and on the other hand the much more doubtful possibilities of some *larger*, even universal, Disarmament consensus which would, however, necessarily involve countries that are not committed, as yet, to such common, minimum principles of World Public Order.

Again, there is a significant new factor introduced into the World Community today by the imminent expansion of the "nuclear club" to include increasingly large numbers of middle and smaller countries not now having nuclear weapons or the technological capacity to produce them. This new danger of widespread nuclear proliferation beyond the "original", Big-Power nuclear states—a horizontal proliferation—is created both by the stockpiling of nuclear weapons by major powers which are already members of the "nuclear club" and which consequently have the ability and the temptation to disseminate such weapons among their military allies and associates; and also by the simplification of the technological processes of manufacture, and the spreading of technical "know-how" as to production, which give more and more countries the possibility of getting into nuclear weapons production on their own independent initiative, with or without Big-Power technical and scientific aid and advice.

The overall dilemma is that that erstwhile nuclear "balance of power" or "balance of terror", stemming from Bipolarity and the twin (Soviet and Western) military bloc systems, and from the relative parity of nuclear weapons and nuclear scientific advances as between the Soviet bloc and the West, has now been displaced. The international law of the Soviet-Western *détente* could perhaps afford to rest on, in a nuclear age, mutual self-restraint and reciprocity of interest, as to the ultimate issues of physical survival and coexistence at least, of the two main contending legal value systems. However, now that the era of political-military Bipolarity seems past, we are dealing instead with widespread fissiparous tendencies within each of the two old political-military blocs and with the consequent emergence of a plurality of new and competing power groupings in the World Community—Polypolarity. A new and properly comprehensive international consensus has yet to emerge that can bind together these disparate power groupings as to minimum conditions of World Public Order for survival in a nuclear age— in replacement of the old, twin-systems' consensus resting on the normative patterns of reciprocal deference between the two blocs that were founded, in the ultimate, on mutual give-and-take and reasonableness and on observance of the Cold War "rules of the game". It is this lack, as yet, of a firmly-based new international consensus, in place of the old consensus of the era of Bipolarity, that renders the task of achieving fundamental accord on Disarmament so difficult but yet so urgent.

In the Soviet-Western dialogue, in the United Nations and elsewhere, over the past few years, concerning the elaboration and refinement of the legal principles of Friendly Relations and Cooperation among States with differing social systems, (Co-existence), Western jurists have consistently urged the eschewing of all the temptations to a general act of Codification of asserted *a priori* legal principles, or holistic formulae generally. Instead, Western jurists have pressed for an essentially low-level, empirically-based approach that would focus on actual problems of Soviet-Western relations, with any general principles to be derived only inductively from those actual cases and their concrete resolution. This pragmatic, empirically-based, problem-oriented, step-by-step, approach to resolution of Soviet-Western conflict was, in effect, quietly accepted by Soviet jurists in the Disarmament area — albeit, accepted *de facto*, if not expressly and in terms. This accounts for the considerable elements of progress actually effected in the Soviet-Western dialogue over Disarmament in the years since the first achievement of the Khrushchev-Kennedy *détente*, with the peaceful resolution of the October, 1962, crisis over the Cuban nuclear missile bases.

The Moscow Partial Test Ban Treaty of August, 1963, was realised and achieved, in its basic conception and drafting at least, through the medium of a Summit Meeting of the nuclear Big Three of that era. But in its actual choice of the content and scope of the ban on nuclear testing that it established, the Treaty reflected the pragmatic approach to international law, in that it sought only the politically possible in terms of then existing Soviet-Western, inter-bloc interests-conflicts. The Soviet-Western accord on the non-orbiting of nuclear weapons in space vehicles, embodied in the U.N. General Assembly Resolution of October 17, 1963 (now incorporated in the new Treaty on Peaceful Uses of Outer Space), was an instance of a concrete follow-up to the Test Ban Treaty's norms, utilising all the political advantages of the step-by-step approach.

Other instances in the area of Disarmament and control of nuclear weapons where these essentially modest, non-rhetorical, gradualist techniques have been amply vindicated by their practical record of results in problem-solving, can be indicated. Premier Khrushchev himself, in an interview given to the United Press International's representative in Moscow in December, 1963, designated certain Soviet and Western moves of this nature, in the Disarmament and related areas, under the phrase "politic of mutual example" — denoting a species of law-making in Soviet-Western relations usually involving a unilateral initiative or lead by one bloc in the confident expectation that the other bloc, by pressure of the world public opinion or the like, would inevitably have to follow. Examples of this "politic of mutual example" can be seen in rapidly successive Soviet and Western decisions as to reduction in arms expenditure, as to the reduction in uranium production, and even the closing of nuclear reactor plants.

On the question of military budgets and also of the size of armed forces, Premier Khrushchev himself suggested that certain measures could "at present be undertaken unilaterally, as a first push, so to speak". Premier Khrushchev, in this regard, in his December, 1963, statement, to United Press International's Moscow representative, announced that the Soviet Union had already adopted a decision as to reduction of military expenditures in the 1964 budget; and he called on other states to do likewise, as a means of relaxation of the arms race and international tension generally, through the "politic of mutual example". It is a fact, of course, that the announcement of the Soviet reductions in arms expenditure was followed almost immediately, in President Johnson's Address to Congress of January 8, 1964, by a similar American announcement of major proportions.

Of equal, if not greater, importance, moreover, was the progress of President Johnson's initiative in the matter of cutbacks in uranium production and in the closing of atomic reactor plants. The U.S. President had accompanied his announcement of the dramatic cuts in the U.S. military budget at the beginning of 1964 by a specific announcement of the curtailment by the United States, in the coming year 1964, of enriched uranium production by 25 per cent, and also of the shutting down of four plutonium piles. President Johnson, at the same time, called on the Soviet Union to follow the American example.

When the Soviet response seemed somewhat slow in coming, the United States renewed the proposal, and made further suggestions not merely that the Soviet Union, in terms, follow the "principle of mutual example" and make similar reductions in its production facilities in fissionable materials, but also that it should agree to the "plant-by-plant shutdown of additional nuclear production facilities on a verified and reciprocal basis". When Premier Khrushchev at last replied to this American invitation, in April, 1964, it was to announce not merely a reduction in Soviet uranium production but also the immediate suspension of the construction of two large new atomic reactors for the production of plutonium.

Thus, for a period of several years after the achievement of the Khrushchev-Kennedy *détente* in October, 1962, with the peaceful resolution of the Cuban missile crisis, the policies — alike the step-by-step approach to resolution of Soviet-Western conflicts, and also of the progression, if need be, by unilateral action relying on its exemplary effect on the other side — were vindicated in a number of vital respects.

It seems a pity, in this regard, that this welcome Soviet-Western momentum has not been maintained and indeed has lagged noticeably recently. Proposals for further, follow-up, measures to those already taken, in terms of a possible joint Soviet-Western freeze on the production of nuclear delivery vehicles, for the destruction, on a reciprocal, Soviet-Western basis, of thousands of nuclear weapons to permit transfer of major quantities of fissionable material to peaceful purposes, and for making a "bonfire" of hundreds of Soviet and American over-age bombers, have — unaccountably, in the light of the promise of the earlier, successful reciprocal Soviet-Western steps — fallen on barren ground. More serious, since not simply a failure to take up some new initiative, but a positive, unilateral reversal or abandonment of an earlier joint initiative, was the announcement by Soviet Finance Minister V. F. Garbuzov, on December 7th, 1965, that the Soviet Union, in the State Budget for 1966, would increase its defense appropriations by five per cent over the previous year, in response to what Mr. Garbuzov characterised as: ". . . an intensification in the activity of the aggressive forces of the imperialist states, a striving on their part to create more and more new hotbeds of war and to restrain the process of social and national liberation by force of arms."

.   .   .

In seeking to establish priorities as to Nuclear Disarmament and Arms Control generally, in an era of World Revolution, the highest priority, clearly, has to be given to achieving a firm and binding international accord on non-proliferation of nuclear weapons. This would mean, necessarily, limiting the "nuclear club" to its present five members — the United States, Soviet Union, Great Britain, France, and Communist China — and, going beyond that, trying to reduce even this limited number of nuclear powers, by progressive steps, in the future. Such a goal would involve, of course, the voluntary abandonment by certain powers of their nuclear weapons and nuclear striking capacity — for example, the lesser nuclear powers, Great Britain, France, and Communist China — in return for adequate alternative guarantees of their territorial security and political independence; and ultimately perhaps the final liquidation of the "nuclear club" by the joint decision of its two original members — the Soviet Union and the United States — according as a really viable international peace-keeping and general security system should be attained. Political realism demands acceptance of the fact that, however much the two main nuclear powers, the Soviet Union and the United States, might recognise their common interest in a staged, step-by-step, mutual progression to complete nuclear disarmament, any Soviet-U.S. ultimate joint decision voluntarily to liquidate the "nuclear club" must necessarily be dependent on achievement of the prior step of abandonment of all nuclear weapons and nuclear striking capacity on the part of the lesser nuclear powers, Great Britain, France, and Communist China; and there is absolutely no evidence, at the present time, of any Communist Chinese interest in doing that, even if the British and the French should be disposed to make the first move.

A correlative, of course, to any international accord on nuclear non-proliferation — which surely must be viewed as a "supereminent" or imperative legal principle, ranking, as *jus cogens*, in hierarchical superiority to other international law principles — must be a legal right of enforcement, on the part of the original parties to any such international accord, against states violating the principle of nuclear non-proliferation (either as donor states, or as receiving states), and this even if the violating states should not themselves be parties or signatories to the original accord.

And related to this principle of nuclear non-proliferation, must be the principle of nuclear non-dissemination, meaning here the obligation of members of the "nuclear club" not to disseminate their nuclear weapons to other, non-nuclear states, even where these latter may be bound to them by military alliance. If the exigencies of military defence should require that the nuclear powers locate some of their nuclear missiles in other states, then it is clearly imperative that such missiles remain at all times under the political and legal authority, and also under the operational control, of the original nuclear power concerned. Failure adequately to accept and apply this principle, on the part of Western political leaders, has been one of the principal obstacles to conclusion of a firm nuclear non-proliferation agreement between the West and the Soviet bloc, in the past few years. The Western political leaders, it is clear, due to bad fact-finding as to basic West German political attitudes, exaggerated the West German desire actually to have nuclear weapons in their own right; and so these Western leaders took too literally former West German Foreign Minister Gerhard Schroeder's insistence on West German access to planning and control of the uses of nuclear weapons, as a condition of West Germany's remaining in NATO and the Western military defence system. It was these Western demands, interpreted (and perhaps over-simplified) by the Soviet leaders as amounting to having a "West German finger on the nuclear trigger", that effectively stalemated the Soviet-Western dialogue over the principle of nuclear non-proliferation. Once the Erhard government had fallen in West Germany, however, and Foreign Minister Schroeder in consequence had been replaced, in December, 1966, the new West German Foreign Minister, Willi Brandt, was able to cut through the several years of equivocation and indirection on the part of the Western political leaders by declaring flatly to the NATO Ministerial Council meeting, that, unlike his predecessor, Dr. Schroeder, he opposed West German participation in an allied nuclear force. The new West German Chancellor, Dr. Kiesinger, seemed to go even further than this in his first policy address, as Chancellor, in the Bundestag, on December 13th, 1966, when he affirmed:

> We shall cooperate in any proposal for armaments control, for a reduction of armaments, and disarmament. The Federal Republic has given an undertaking to its partners in the alliance to renounce the production of atomic weapons, and has in that respect submitted to international control. We seek neither national control nor national ownership of atomic weapons.

Actually, right from the outset, Foreign Minister Schroeder's aspirations to nuclear weapons for West Germany, in its own right, had been both militarily unnecessary in view of the advanced nuclear striking power already existing, under American control, in the American NATO bases in West Germany; and also politically unrealistic, even foolish, since exacerbating West German relations with the Soviet Union and so further delaying any prospects of German political reunification. Now that the new West German Foreign Minister, Willi Brandt, has apparently officially repudiated any West German pretensions to nuclear weapons, it may be hoped that the last has been heard, on the part of Western political leaders generally, of any question of German access, direct or indirect, to nuclear weapons or nuclear weapon planning and control. Our past policy on this question has, I think, been one of the major Western political mistakes and errors of judgment, of the years since President Kennedy's death.

Actually, the over-riding importance of ensuring that rational decision-making shall apply in any ultimate decision to use nuclear weapons requires that every step be taken to avoid having nuclear weapons fall into "non-rational" hands, outside the original members of the "nuclear club"; and that dissemination of nuclear weapons outside their own countries be avoided by the original nuclear powers, even where such dissemination may involve retention of their own authority and control. This proposition leads on, more or less inevitably, to the conclusion that the creation, and progressive extension, of nuclear-free zones — in Latin America, Africa, the Middle East, and Central Europe — must be one of the major priorities in the step-by-step approach to general nuclear disarmament. In this regard, the Rapacki Plan — named after the Polish Foreign Minister who first advanced it — providing for the withdrawal of nuclear weapons from West Germany, East Germany, Poland, and Czechoslovakia, was perhaps too cursorily and peremptorily dismissed by Western political leaders, without proper consideration of its affirmative merits and advantages, for the Soviet bloc and the West equally, as an instrument for reducing political tension and also the danger of nuclear escalation in Central Europe. By the same token, however, the detailed proposals by the then West German Chancellor, Ludwig Erhard, of March 25th, 1966, directed towards an East-West standstill agreement on the number of nuclear weapons maintained in Europe, and directed also to their ultimate reduction, by stages, were perhaps too quickly dismissed by Soviet political leaders.

Allied to the Rapacki Plan must be various concrete proposals for the alleviation of political-military tension in Central Europe. The disturbed political condition of Central Europe after the War, and the legally unresolved territorial and boundary questions, were principal factors in triggering the post-war arms race and also the nuclear confrontation of the original, Cold War era. The sympathetic consideration given by President Johnson's White House Conference on International Co-operation, in November and December, 1965, to the idea of a non-aggression pact between NATO and the Warsaw Pact Organisation — allied to similar initiatives from time to time among the Soviet Bloc countries of Eastern Europe that look, indeed, to the eventual dissolution of both political-military organisations — offers a most promising approach to alleviation of tensions in a particular geographical, "tinder-box", area, which, so long as its problems remain unresolved, will always present the possibility of an escalation into nuclear war. Any such resolution of Central European problems must, of course, make appropriate reconciliation of the interest in security of territorial boundaries and of settled expectations on the one hand, and the interest in self-determination of peoples on the other. But such a reconciliation seems eminently possible and reasonable, if the over-riding, common Soviet-Western, interest in reducing the threat of nuclear war be kept in mind.

If, of course, the non-nuclear states are persuaded, or otherwise constrained, to give up their own claims (based on the arguments of the principle of sovereign equality of states, both nuclear and non-nuclear, and the further principle of equal rights), to develop or acquire nuclear weapons, then the nuclear powers seem reciprocally obligated to guarantee these non-nuclear states against the threat or use of force against their territorial integrity or political independence; and this whether such force involves use of nuclear or of conventional means of warfare. All this, of course, gives greater urgency than ever to the development of effective international peace-keeping institutions and procedures, under the aegis of the United Nations or otherwise.

Beyond this, the nuclear powers seem to have at least a moral obligation to take steps for the transfer, for peaceful (non-military) use of determinate quantities of U-235 and other fissionable materials, for the benefit of the "new" or developing countries. Such transfers should, preferably, be effected through the International Atomic Energy Agency, with appropriate safeguards to ensure only peaceful, non-military, use by the receiving country.

The emphasis on nuclear disarmament and nuclear arms control must not obscure the need for control of conventional, non-nuclear, arms build-up, on the part not merely of the nuclear powers but also of other states. The imaginative leads given by both the United States and the Soviet Union in recent years in the staged, reciprocal cutbacks in the size of their overall military budgets — plus the various, as yet only inchoate, proposals for a "bonfire" of over-age bombers and other military aircraft — are examples of the ways in which significant progress can be made, through use of step-by-step methods, in the reduction of conventional, as well as nuclear, armaments. It is a pity, in this regard, that the "politic of (Soviet-U.S.) mutual example", as applied in progressive, percentage-wise cutbacks in the size of military budgets, from year to year, seems now to have lapsed, beginning with the year 1966.

The *political* problems of nuclear and general disarmament may seem ever greater, from year to year, in view of that expansion of the original "nuclear club" that has already taken place, disturbing the original two-party, balance of rationality; and in view also of the imminent prospect of far wider, and ultimately, perhaps, near-universal, membership of the "nuclear club", unless some effective international control on this be soon applied. However, by way of some compensation, the *technical*, scientific problems of nuclear and general disarmament, for their part, are benefiting by continuing advances in scientific technology. Recent scientific breakthroughs in national detection systems, for example, involving use of advanced techniques for underground, seismic observation, have immensely facilitated the task of effective monitoring of the observance of any future international agreement extending the Moscow Partial Test Ban Treaty of August, 1963, so as to interdict underground nuclear explosions. These scientific advances, as President Johnson's White House Conference on International Cooperation, in late 1965, recognised, tend to minimise for the future (though not perhaps actually to eliminate altogether) the need for physical, on-the-site, inspection and verification procedures. The insistence on such physical, on-the-site, inspection and verification procedures, on the part of the West, in the detailed nuclear disarmament discussions at the United Nations and at Geneva, in the years since President Kennedy's death, has been a major obstacle to any further agreement, with the Soviet Union, extending the Moscow Test Ban Treaty to the forbidding of underground nuclear tests. Of course, this stubborn Western insistence, in retrospect, may have been perfectly rational and justifiable in the light of then existing scientific knowledge; and, likewise, the Soviet objection to such on-the-site verification procedures may have, for its part, unnecessarily sought to defer to old-fashioned, essentially nineteenth century, notions of State sovereignty. Nevertheless, it is refreshing and encouraging to have confirmed, in this striking way, the extent to which scientific progress can itself help in eliminating problems of more strictly juridical discord and disagreement between the main legal systems of the contemporary World Community. In this way, the continuing scientific, technological, revolution of our time, by constantly developing new techniques and procedures for controlling erstwhile insoluble old problems, aids and facilitates the peaceful resolution of the various legacies of the ideological revolution of our time.

*New Frontiers for Science, and
the Competing Ideologies*

The doctrine of "Peaceful Coexistence" represented the *leit-motiv* of Soviet foreign policy in the period, after the official inauguration of the de-Stalinisation campaign in 1956, when Premier Khrushchev assumed political leadership in the Soviet Union. In his address to the 22nd Congress of the Communist Party, on October 17th, 1961, Premier Khrushchev assured his audience of top-level Soviet decision-makers that the principles of Peaceful Coexistence, whose ultimate source he attributed to Lenin, had "always been the central feature of Soviet foreign policy". Premier Khrushchev had coupled his remarks on Peaceful Coexistence with a call for more extensive business relations with all countries, among which he specifically listed Britain, France, Italy, West Germany, and other West European countries. Peaceful Coexistence and Peaceful Economic Competition, as identified by Premier Khrushchev, were thus firmly linked as the two major elements in the post-Stalin era, Soviet diplomatic and political offensive in the West and in the neutralist, Third World. Apart from its significance, in the Khrushchev era, in what might be called the polemics of Soviet-Western relations, the subject of Peaceful Coexistence, in terms, had been on the agenda, and had also been extensively debated, at all the biennial reunions, since 1956, of the authoritative International Law Association — the World-wide, scientific association of international lawyers that has always managed to transcend the frontiers of the two main ideological blocs, Communist and Capitalist. Beyond this, the United Nations General Assembly, at its 17th session in the Fall of 1962, included Peaceful

Coexistence on its agenda, albeit under the somewhat inelegant, Western-sponsored euphemism of "Friendly Relations and Cooperation Among States": under this same title, Peaceful Coexistence has been debated exhaustively at every regular session of the U.N. General Assembly since that time, and has been made the subject of two special United Nations conferences, held at Mexico City in the Fall of 1964 and in New York in the Spring of 1966. The official purpose of these protracted Soviet-Western debates over Coexistence, whether in the scientific arena of the International Law Association, or in the political arena of the U.N. General Assembly, has been to elaborate the detailed, concrete, secondary principles which alone could give meaning and content to the essentially abstract generality of the concept of Coexistence itself.

It must be noted, that, from the outset, even in Soviet juristic thinking, Peaceful Coexistence always had a somewhat ambivalent character. Thus, in one sense, in Premier Khrushchev's own words, uttered in January, 1961, some months before his address to the 22nd Congress of the Communist Party already referred to, Premier Khrushchev explained the policy of Peaceful Coexistence to a Soviet audience as being no more than a "form of intensive economic, political and ideological struggle of the proletariat against the aggressive forces of imperialism in the international arena": I think, here, that Premier Khrushchev was appealing to that hard-line, neo-Stalinist remnant of Soviet juristic thinking which would use peaceful coexistence as no more than a convenient camouflage for achieving "proletarian internationalism" in the special sense of coordinated world revolution — in effect, using it as a sort of "Trojan horse" device to lull Western suspicions while the Soviet Union might proceed quietly with preparations (again, in one of Premier Khrushchev's colourful phrases) "to bury the West".

On the other hand, in its development in Premier Khrushchev's own personal thinking, as increasingly evidenced in the empirical record of the facts of Soviet foreign policy-in-action in the period of Premier Khrushchev's leadership, Peaceful Coexistence came increasingly to take on the aspect of a somewhat static, conservative, even reactionary doctrine — somewhat redolent of Metternich and the post–Congress of Vienna "Holy

Alliance" attempts to stifle political liberalism and political change in the name of the principle of "legitimacy". In effect, in this particular orientation, Soviet foreign policy, in the era of Premier Khrushchev, became increasingly interested in the possibility, by bilateral arrangements or understandings with the West, of consecrating the political and military balance of power in the World, as a formal juridical condition. For Peaceful Coexistence, in this sense, would amount virtually to a legitimation of the political and military *status quo* of the Cold War era. Insofar as it would accept the factual, existential condition of the Cold War bi-polar division of the World into the two great military blocs dominated respectively by the Soviet Union and the United States, it would necessarily concede general control and responsibility by each bloc leader over its own sphere of influence. It would further proclaim a principle of non-interference by either the Soviet Union or the United States in the other's bloc, however great the temptation to profit by the other side's difficulties at any time might be, and however great the moral anguish at not being able to intervene in specific cases. We had this demonstrated most dramatically, as far as the West was concerned, in the frustrations of the West's own, self-imposed, restraint in the Berlin and East German riots of 1953, and most tragically, certainly, in the events in Hungary in the Fall of 1956. By the same token, Premier Khrushchev must have experienced some of the West's bitter frustration over Berlin and over Hungary, in the circumstances surrounding the Soviet Union's withdrawal, in the Fall of 1962 — once President Kennedy had responded resolutely — from its Cuban adventure that had been initiated, in the preceding Summer, with the clandestine emplacement of Soviet offensive, ground-to-ground, nuclear missiles in Cuba. This is what was meant, in the somewhat cynical Cold War vernacular of the time, by speaking of a Soviet-Western understanding to "balance" Hungary and Cuba.

Such is the development in Soviet-Western "friendly relations", in the years since the peaceful resolution of the Cuban missile crisis, that while, once, the standard Western interpretation of Soviet foreign policy under the rubric of Peaceful Coexistence was the first, or hard-line approach, today it is fairly generally accepted by Western jurists that a practical, working, *détente* exists between the Soviet Union and the West, and that the Soviet Union is as genuinely interested, as we are ourselves, in further elaborating and concretising and extending that *détente*. Part of the credit for this change must go to Western scientific lawyers who took part in the detailed debates, in the late 1950s and the early 1960s, in the International Law Association, with Soviet and Soviet bloc lawyers. Anticipating or transcending the intellectual positions taken by more cautious or timorous official legal spokesmen in Western foreign ministries, these "legal laymen", so to speak, pressed their Soviet counterparts to be specific and concrete, and to discuss actual problem-situations. I can remember the stormy debate over Peaceful Coexistence at the Brussels reunion of the International Law Association, in August, 1962 — only two months before the Cuban missile crisis. The head of the Soviet legal delegation — the then Principal Legal Adviser to the Soviet Foreign Ministry — had virtually threatened to walk out because Western lawyers insisted, for their part, that it was not enough to talk of Co-existence in terms of cloudy generalities formulated always at a very high level of abstraction. Western lawyers suggested, instead, that the Soviet-Western legal dialogue could only usefully be conducted by eschewing bitter, and largely futile, debate over questions of political theory and ideology, and concentrating instead on current tension-situations of Soviet-Western relations and the immediate range of practical solutions available for them. Here was the genesis of that pragmatic, empirical, problem-oriented, step-by-step approach to solution of Soviet-Western conflicts that was to be so strikingly vindicated, a year later, by its direct employment as the operational methodology for achieving the Moscow Partial Test Ban Treaty of August, 1963. It was the quiet, *de facto* acceptance of this same scientific method, on the part of Soviet jurists (including, by the way, the then Principal Legal Adviser to the Soviet Foreign Ministry, the very able and balanced Professor Gregory Tunkin), — in the place of the old-line, *a priori*, absolutistic approach that had stressed the only way to resolution of Soviet-Western conflicts as being through the postulation, in one comprehensive law-making act, of a universal, general Code of Principles of Peaceful Coexistence — that for the first time really permitted joint, cooperative, Soviet-Western scientific effort towards the ending of the Cold War and the relief of international tensions in practical ways.

The emphasis on concrete problem-solving, in Soviet-Western relations, and on the practical breakthrough achieved by replacing ideological debate (which so often in the past has ended up in name-calling and trading of insults) by empirically-based methods, calls attention to the fact that in the more technical, scientific areas, the element of Soviet-Western cooperation, or at least recognition of common interest, has always been present — even before the political *détente* of Premier Khrushchev and President Kennedy had been achieved. In fact, going beyond this, we might say that the most promising way to a genuine Soviet-Western cooperation in the future, transcending the somewhat negative condition of Coexistence inaugurated by the political *détente*, is through the approach to technical, scientific problems. For here all the evidence of the record of Soviet-Western relations of the past few years suggests that the more demanding and difficult the problem, in scientific terms, the greater the degree of Soviet and Western mutuality and reciprocity of interest is likely to be; and that it is the scientists themselves (construing this term in the broadest sense to include social scientists, as well as natural or physical scientists), who are best equipped, on both sides, to secure or facilitate fundamental Soviet-Western accords or understandings in these areas, since less bothered by the ideological preconceptions and *a priori* moral judgments which have generally so preoccupied or frustrated the professional diplomats from the respective foreign ministries in the past.

I can illustrate this by reference to substantial practical achievements in Soviet-Western understanding and cooperation — in highly technical areas demanding high technical skills for their understanding — at times when, at a more strictly political level, further progress in ameliorating Soviet-Western relations might not have seemed very promising.

First, we may refer to the problem of the peaceful exploration and development of Antarctica. The United States Department of State, in 1948, realising the inevitable drift towards international conflict because of the welter of rival national territorial claims in Antarctica, had taken the diplomatic initiative and had proposed to the countries then having competing or overlapping claims to territorial sovereignty in Antarctica — Argentina, Chile, France, Norway, Great Britain, Australia, and New Zealand — the desirability of calling an international conference looking towards possible internationalisation of Antarctica. The reaction of the seven states so approached, however, was generally hostile to any surrender of national claims, and so the matter had to be dropped. At this stage, the Soviet Union came into the picture for the first time, demanding full participation in any Antarctic settlement. The U.S. State Department had not, of course, included the Soviet Union in its list of interested states, 1948 being the year, by most counts, of the inception of the Cold War. Following on the Soviet bid, matters were allowed to drift for some years, though the question of Antarctica was proposed by India for discussion at the U.N. General Assembly in the Fall of 1956.

The maturing of the plans for the International Geophysical Year, however, brought Antarctica back, as a subject for international scientific discussion, and also brought full-scale Soviet involvement. The International Geophysical Year, or IGY, was planned and administered by a special committee of the International Council of Scientific Unions. Though in some countries, and particularly those of the Soviet bloc, the scientific societies and academies are wholly or partly government-controlled, the emphasis has been so clearly scientific that the Council, in the view of competent Western observers, has been able to preserve a relatively independent, non-governmental character. The Antarctic figured prominently in the Council's programme for IGY, right from the outset. Regional conferences on the Antarctic, in connection with IGY, were held from 1955 onwards, with the Soviet Union sending official delegates and taking a leading part throughout.

There was genuine concern, at the time, that the Cold War might be extended to the South Pole, particularly since the Soviet Union had been assigned base sites and IGY responsibilities in the territorial sector of Antarctica claimed by Australia. During this period, governments were being urged from many sides to take steps to assure their own national claims in Antarctica; but at the same time there remained the countervailing scientifically-based interests in maintaining freedom of enquiry in the Antarctic continent. The IGY, in this sense, was a scientist-conceived and scientist-developed programme, operating under the clear understanding of all the scientists from the various national groups — Soviet bloc, Western, and "uncommitted" — that all activities conducted during IGY, that is, to the end of 1958, would be politically neutral in the sense of involving absolutely no ruling, one way or another, as to the legal character of existing claims to territorial sovereignty in Antarctica. Now while, prior to the Soviet participation in IGY, it would clearly have been possible, *legally*, to conclude a general international treaty providing for a final settlement of the political status of Antarctica, limited to those Western countries that, alone, at that time had international law–based territorial claims in that region, any such agreement had been *politically* impossible because of the welter of competing Western claims and the mutual intransigence of those same Western countries in what was, after all, a non–Cold War issue. After the Soviet participation in IGY and the Soviet programme of scientific work in Antarctica as part of that participation, an Antarctic *régime* for the future that would exclude the Soviet Union had clearly become politically, if not indeed legally, impossible.

The next political moves as to Antarctica were clearly designed to build upon the era of international, inter-systems, Soviet and Western, good feeling that had permeated the multinational effort in Antarctica during the IGY. Some months prior to the termination of IGY at the end of 1958, the American President, President Eisenhower, had foreshadowed a dramatically new approach to regulation of the Antarctic continent. In President Eisenhower's own words:

> The United States is dedicated to the principle that the vast uninhabited wastes of Antarctica shall be used only for peaceful purposes. We do not want Antarctica to become an object of political conflict . . . .
>
> We propose that Antarctica shall be open to all nations to conduct scientific or other peaceful activities there. We also propose that joint administrative arrangements be worked out . . . .

President Eisenhower then proceeded to invite a group of

twelve countries, comprising, among others, all existing territorial claimants to Antarctica, plus the Soviet Union, and finally also Japan (which had itself formally renounced any territorial pretensions to Antarctica, in the World War II Peace Treaty of 1951), to take part in an international conference in Washington designed, essentially, to permit a direct transition from IGY to a new international *régime* of Antarctica. Some fifteen months of discussions then ensued, characterised by a substantial maintenance of the inter-systems goodwill and cooperation that had been so notable throughout IGY. The chief Soviet delegate to the Washington conference on Antarctica, Mr. Kuznetsov, expressed, from the outset, the Soviet Union's interest in settling the question of the *régime* for Antarctica on an international basis. The final outcome of the conference was the Antarctic Treaty, which was signed in Washington on December 1st, 1959.

The Preamble to the new Treaty expressly recited both the "substantial contributions to scientific knowledge resulting from international cooperation in scientific investigation in Antarctica"; and also the fact of the "establishment of a firm foundation for the continuation and development of such cooperation on the basis of freedom of scientific investigation in Antarctica as applied during the International Geophysical Year".

The key operational provisions of the Antarctic Treaty of 1959, for our present purposes, are Articles 1, 3, 5 and 7.

Article 1 provides:

"Antarctica shall be used for peaceful purposes only. There shall be prohibited, *inter alia*, any measures of a military nature, such as the establishment of military bases and fortifications, the carrying out of military manoeuvres, as well as the testing of any type of weapons."

Article 5, in the same spirit (and anticipating, by four years, the Moscow Partial Test Ban Treaty of the Summer of 1963), declares: "Any nuclear explosions in Antarctica and the disposal there of radioactive waste material shall be prohibited."

It is in Article 3 of the Treaty, however, that that spirit of positive international scientific cooperation, transcending the ideological frontiers of the then existing political-military blocs, that was so successfully established in the International Geophysical Year, is captured and extended. Article 3 provides for the exchange of information regarding plans for scientific programmes in Antarctica; for the exchange of scientific personnel between different national expeditions and stations in Antarctica; and for the exchange of scientific observations and the results of scientific investigations and researches. This is concretely followed up in Article 7 of the Treaty which provides for the designation of national observers, with authority to carry out detailed inspections of all areas of Antarctica, including all stations, installations and equipment, and all ships and aircraft, and which also permits aerial observation — all this designed to ensure the proper carrying out of the provisions of the Treaty.

It remains to say that the Antarctic Treaty remains in full practical working operation to this day, without any serious complaint as to violation of its terms or its essential spirit. The patterns of concrete Soviet-Western, inter-systems cooperation in a technical, scientific area where Soviet-Western long-range self-interest was essentially the same and not conflicting, were followed, four years later, in the successful Soviet-Western negotiations leading to the conclusion of the Moscow Test Ban Treaty of August, 1963. We have already discussed the Moscow Test Ban Treaty in earlier lectures. It is only necessary to note, now, that while the Khrushchev-Kennedy *détente* resulting from the peaceful, and essentially amicable, settlement of the Soviet-Western crisis of October, 1962, over the emplacement of Soviet offensive nuclear missiles in Cuba, may have provided the political opportunity for proceeding to discussion and negotiation of the principle of banning nuclear weapon tests in the atmosphere, in outer space, and under water, it was the weight of scientific evidence, on both sides, Soviet and Western, as to the general danger to human life resulting from nuclear fall-out and nuclear radiation unless such weapon testing were soon halted, that succeeded in communicating an especial sense of urgency to the political leaders' attempt to reach a firm Soviet-Western agreement and settlement on this point. The common danger that itself, of course, acknowledged no ideological frontier, and that was amply attested to by the scientists from both main ideological systems, thus led inevitably to common acceptance of the principle of control of nuclear weapon testing, in the form of a firm international legal accord resting on the inter-systems consensus.

The Moscow Test Ban Treaty of August, 1963, had, among other things, dealt tangentially with the problem of peaceful regulation of Outer Space, insofar as the ban on nuclear weapon testing that it established extended also to Outer Space. At the United Nations in early December of 1966, it was finally announced that agreement had been reached on the text of a comprehensive treaty governing the peaceful regulation of Outer Space and Space Exploration. The text of the treaty, which consists of a preamble and seventeen articles, had been worked out in the United Nations Committee on the Peaceful Uses of Outer Space and its expert legal sub-committee of twenty-eight members headed by Professor Manfred Lachs, the distinguished Polish international lawyer who followed up this activity by being chosen, by a near unanimous vote, as a judge of the World Court at the elections held in the United Nations in the Fall of 1966. The text of the treaty, as worked out in the Committee, was promptly approved by the United Nations General Assembly; and it was then opened for signature by individual states. The treaty itself was to come into effect, according to its own Article 14, upon ratification by five governments (which were to include the Soviet Union, the United Kingdom, and the United States), a legal condition expected to be successfully completed as early as January of 1967.

The immediate negotiations at the United Nations, leading to the new, agreed text, lasted almost six months; though they had been preceded by a number of years of difficulty and protracted and seemingly fruitless discussions between lawyers and scientific experts from the Soviet Union and the United States and other countries. Agreement, though, had become certain — barring, of course, any unexpected major political development marring then existing Soviet–United States relations, such as a really marked or unexpected step-up in the American military escalation in the Vietnam War — at that moment, in June of 1966, when, within a day of each other, first the Soviet Union and then the United States filed with the Secretary-General of the United Nations almost identical texts for a draft treaty on Space. The Soviet version was for a treaty "On principles governing the activities of States in the exploration and use of Outer Space, the Moon, and other Celestial Bodies"; while the American version was for a treaty "governing the exploration of the Moon and other Celestial Bodies".

The final, agreed treaty text, as approved by the U.N. Committee and then, formally, by the U.N. General Assembly in December, 1966, declares, in its opening Article:

> The exploration and use of Outer Space, including the moon and other celestial bodies, shall be carried out for the benefit and in the interests of all countries, irrespective of their degree of economic or scientific development.

The same article, Article 1, goes on to affirm that: "Outer Space, including the moon and other celestial bodies, shall be free for exploration and use by all states without discrimination of any kind"; and that "there shall be free access to all areas of celestial bodies", and "freedom of scientific investigation in Outer Space".

The main operative provisions of the new treaty are contained, however, in two articles. Article (2) proclaims:

> Outer Space, including the moon and other celestial bodies, is not subject to national appropriation by claim of sovereignty, by means of use or occupation, or by any other means.

Article (4) reads as follows:

> States parties to the treaty undertake not to place in orbit around the earth any objects carrying nuclear weapons or any other kinds of weapons of mass destruction, install such weapons on celestial bodies, or station such weapons in Outer Space in any other manner.

The same article, Article 4, goes on to declare that "the moon and other celestial bodies shall be used . . . exclusively for peaceful purposes"; and that "the establishment of military bases" and "the testing of any type of weapons" is to be forbidden, — though not, however, the "use of military personnel for scientific research or for any other peaceful purposes".

When one looks at these two articles — the principal sum of the constructive achievement of the new Space treaty — one must acknowledge that, from the international law viewpoint, the new treaty probably does not break too much new legal ground.

The orbiting of nuclear weapons in Space vehicles, for example, was expressly prohibited by the United Nations General Assembly Resolution of October 17th, 1963, which had been passed, originally, with joint Soviet and American backing. This had been one of the fruits of that Khrushchev-Kennedy, joint Soviet-American, *détente* that had followed so closely on the peaceful resolution of the October, 1962, crisis over the Soviet emplacement of offensive nuclear missiles in Cuba, and that had been highlighted by the successful achievement and signing of the Moscow Nuclear Test Ban Treaty in August, 1963. Though there may be some rather formalistic international lawyers who may still deny the effect of law to a United Nations General Assembly Resolution even where it rests, as here, on the consensus of all the main competing political and social systems of the World, for most of the World Community the Resolution on non-orbiting of nuclear weapons had been accepted as being binding international law from the moment of its adoption in the United Nations. And, of course, this particular principle has been fully observed in the spirit and in the letter in the more than three years since that time.

As for the notion that the moon and other celestial bodies should not be subject to national appropriation or national sovereignty, that principle had been expressly conceded by Soviet international lawyers, in the Soviet-Western debates and discussions taking place, over a number of years, at the biennial reunions of the authoritative, if private, International Law Association; and also in Soviet scientific legal writings on Space. The Soviet opinions on this issue were the more interesting because first advanced at a time when, by all accounts, the Soviet Union had a head start on the West in Space exploration and therefore seemed more likely than anyone else to be able to try to apply customary international law rules as to territorial ownership and title, to the moon at least.

In the end, I think, the importance of the new Space treaty lies not so much in any legal novelty of the principles now finally expressed in treaty form, but in two things. First, the achievement of a firm treaty text on Space confirms what has been apparent to students of Soviet-Western relations over a number of years, that in matters of a high scientific character where both main bloc leaders, the Soviet Union and the United States, tend to have achieved approximately the same level of technical development and advancement, it is not too difficult to record these facts in a formal agreement that is rested firmly upon mutuality and reciprocity of interests as between the two systems, Soviet and American. Hence, for example, the Moscow Test Ban Treaty of August, 1963; and hence, also, the original agreement of 1959 upon Antarctica, providing both for its non-military use and also for scientific cooperation in its exploration.

The second, and by far the most significant reason for the importance of the new Space treaty at the present time, is that it is the first really substantial breakthrough, of a formally recognised and publicly acknowledged character, in Soviet-Western relations, since the Moscow Test Ban Treaty of August, 1963, and the United Nations General Assembly Resolution on non-orbiting of nuclear weapons in Space vehicles of October, 1963.

The high hopes engendered by both these measures for a pragmatic, empirical, step-by-step progression to further concretisation of that Khrushchev-Kennedy *détente* which the peaceful resolution of the Cuban missile crisis of October, 1962, had begun, were shattered by President Kennedy's assassination in Dallas in late November, 1963, and by Premier Khrushchev's abrupt dismissal from office the following year. The intervening three years have been rather bleak from the viewpoint of *formal*, inter-systems accords going to fundamental issues of conflict, as new and apparently personally less sympathetic individuals than Khrushchev and Kennedy succeeded to office in both the Soviet Union and in the West, and as Soviet–United States relations grew progressively colder as the United States involvement in Vietnam deepened. Does this latest Soviet-Western accord and understanding on Space, taken in conjunction with the marked worsening of Chinese-Soviet relations, suggest that both the Soviet Union and the United States have decided that, in spite of any personal antipathies or dislikes among their respective leaders, the time has come to try to re-establish and to extend the Khrushchev-Kennedy *détente* once more, on a concrete basis of formal, inter-systems accords? If so, given some new wit and imagination and *élan* on the part of Western leaders, and for that matter also some reasonable spirit of cooperation on the part of Soviet leaders, the new agreement on Space could be merely the first in a rapid series of Soviet-Western agreements, designed to end some of the old quarrels of the old era of ideological conflict, at long last. Among these, the non-proliferation and non-dissemination of nuclear weapons to countries not now having them; the establishment of nuclear free zones in Central Europe, the Middle East, Africa, Latin America; a final peace treaty and settlement of territorial boundaries in Central Europe; a non-aggression pact between NATO and the Warsaw Pact countries, — seem merely the most urgent problems among many in which, objectively viewed, the interests of the Soviet Union and the West in a final solution seem substantially identical. And so firm international agreements, granted mutual common-sense and mutual reasonableness, should not be impossible of achievement.

THE "WINDS OF CHANGE" IN THE WORLD COMMUNITY, AND WORLD PUBLIC ORDER

In the latest, 1964, edition of the main Soviet textbook on international law, edited by Professor Kozhevnikov who was himself, very briefly, the Soviet judge on the World Court, Western conceptions of the nature and basic character of international . law, are severely criticised. As the Soviet textbook contends:

> The bourgeois juristic science limited itself, as a rule, only to formal dogmatic definitions of international law. It is not in condition to reveal its essence, class nature and social purpose in the contemporary epoch.

Now while we would certainly not, in the West, be disposed to agree with Professor Kozhevnikov and his colleagues' conclusion, from this, that it is possible to explain the essence of contemporary international law only on a basis of the principles of Marxism-Leninism, nevertheless intellectual candour does compel us to admit that too much of Western international legal science has been devoted — as one of the more intellectually imaginative of the contemporary American jurists, Myres McDougal, has complained — to an "over-emphasis on technical rules unrelated to policies as factors in guiding and shaping decisions". For the old-line Western legal theories looked, not to the substantive policy content of a claimed rule of law, but to the various formal categories of official sources of international law to which it might be allocated. In a word, the fundamental enquiry for purposes of deciding whether a claimed rule really deserved the accolade of being called international law was not what was in it, meaning whether, intrinsically, it was a sensible or fair rule, but where it came from, meaning whether it was one or other of custom, treaty, and the like.

One can understand that for jurists trained in the positivistic theories of law (as so many Western lawyers have been), where law is viewed, in Austinian terms, as being command, without regard to its moral content, as such, the identification of a claimed rule in terms of its "source" alone, may be enough to complete the process of enquiry as to whether it really is international law. This is the more so since these same jurists come from national legal systems that have themselves actively participated, in past eras, in the process of historical formation of rules of customary international law, and in the actual negotiation and elaboration of treaty-based international law — so that presumably their own national self-interest has been fully consulted in the creation or definition of those same rules.

Yet this is hardly true in the case of the "new" countries that succeeded to independence and self-government in the wake of the collapse of the old Colonial empires in Asia and Africa, or for that matter in the case of the post-1918 "succession states" that came into being after the downfall of the old Imperial dynasties in Central and Eastern Europe. For these countries, the crucial question is likely to be whether, in terms of the contemporary World Community, a claimed rule of international law is a good rule or a bad rule — to be ascertained by the extent to which the claimed rule maximises the various competing interests being pressed in the World Community. The argument from age alone is, in this context, hardly likely to be very persuasive. Age, by itself, is surely neutral; for one used, once, to burn witches under the authority of the positive law. Mr. Justice Oliver Wendell Holmes, Jr., of the United States Supreme Court used to say that it was revolting to have no more substantial justification for a claimed legal rule than that it was so laid down in the time of Henry IV. It is perhaps this same philosophy that is represented by the comment by the Soviet jurist Professor Gregory Tunkin to the question of the extent to which the "new", Afro-Asian countries are bound by old rules of customary international law that were created before they came into political existence: Professor Tunkin's own suggestion is that any rule of international law that is sought to be based on "custom" must satisfy the double standard of not merely being satisfactorily evidenced through historical practice of States, but also of being actually "accepted" by States. Professor Tunkin thus makes the agreement of States — if you wish, inter-systems consensus — the essence of the process of creation of norms of international law.

Does this mean that all claimed principles of international law must be subjected to a sort of international "rule of reason", before they can be admitted as being normative and binding at the present day? There was a time, perhaps, when Soviet jurists seemed bent on rejecting the whole corpus of traditional or classical international law — or at least pre-1917 international law — as being *per se* outdated and without any juridical effect and significance in present-day terms. Yet any thoughts of a resultant condition of legal anarchy in the World Community must be tempered by consideration of more recent Soviet juristic writings. Western international lawyers, remembering, with Mr. Justice Oliver Wendell Holmes, Jr., that the life of the law has not been logic but experience, will certainly approve of Professor Tunkin's recent statement that the "science of law, like all other sciences, must base itself on facts, the facts of international life". Again, we can hardly do less than welcome Professor Tunkin's public recognition of the continued juridical viability today of "old democratic fundamental principles of international law". The overall trend in evidence in Professor Tunkin's most recent published writings, in fact, is one of a skilful attempt at increasing approximation or assimilation of Soviet international-law thinking to more generally accepted, orthodox or classical, doctrine. When Professor Tunkin joined issue in public with Sir Francis Vallat, the Legal Adviser to the British Foreign Office, for example, it was to insist that what he, Professor Tunkin, was advocating was "new international law" only; and that he certainly had called "neither for 'a new international law' nor for a 'revolution' in international law". And so, Professor Tunkin has been at pains to stress that Soviet jurists have "no intention of overthrowing the international law now in force".

It seems to me that what Professor Tunkin is saying, here, — and he was speaking at the time that he was still the Principal Legal Adviser to the Soviet Foreign Ministry, prior to his recent election as Professor Korovin's successor in the Chair of International Law at Moscow — is that the need today is for a more or less evolutionary international law-making that would, however, accept the existing corpus of classical international law doctrine as the necessary minimum starting point for legal innovation and for creative adaptation of old rules and principles to new political, social, and economic conditions in the World Community. Such a juridical approach has, of course, a very great deal in common with those Western-based intellectual attitudes, stemming from the Legal Realist and Sociological schools of thinking, that would eschew old-fashioned positivistic, law-as-command, approaches to law, in favour of detailed, empirically-based study of the *de facto* claims and interests being pressed in international society at any particular time; and that would accept also the conception of a positive law that changes, in measure, as society itself, and the complex of interests represented in it, themselves change. On this approach, the most remarkable feature of the state of international law, in the era since the Khrushchev-Kennedy *détente*, has been the demonstration, again and again, of the degree of common, Soviet bloc and Western, interest in so many of its rules and principles. For very many, if not the great bulk, of the principles of the old, classical international law continue to be viable today, since resting on clear mutuality and reciprocity of interest as between the two great social and economic systems, Soviet and Western.

To explain this startling fact, after the fiery polemics of the Soviet-Western debate during the Cold War years when Stalin was in full command in the Soviet Union, is to recognise several important truths. First the acceptance of the pragmatic, empirically-based, problem-oriented, step-by-step approach to resolution of Soviet-Western conflicts meant a replacement of the erstwhile *a priori* absolutism on both sides in favour of scientific problem-solving; and the very de-ideologisation of the conflict facilitated and accelerated common solutions, since enabling focussing on the actual problem itself and the range of alternative solutions available, uncluttered by the rival philosophical preconceptions or by Cold War propaganda in general. But the very de-ideologisation of the Soviet-Western conflict, and the increasing revelation, to both sides, that they would tend to identify the really significant problems in the same way and also to reach the same essential conclusions as to the best solutions for those problems, are themselves a consequence, in considerable measure, of the marked social and economic advances in the Soviet Union in recent years; of the increasing approximation of Soviet industrial strength and Soviet economic production to Western levels; and of the progressive *embourgeoisement* not merely of the actual Soviet decision-making cadre, but also of the managerial and technocratic personnel and the intelligentsia generally. Societies at relatively similar stages of social and economic development tend to have the same general problems and tend also to employ the same social controls or legal remedies to resolve them, whether according to Soviet scientific Marxism in its modern empirical form as represented by the new generation of Soviet jurists, or according to Western-based sociological jurisprudence. It is hardly surprising, in this regard, that the Soviet Union should be increasingly concerned with more traditional legal values involving historical continuity and predictability in legal development, and also stability of and due deference to settled expectations of the sort that any mature legal system, whether in the international or a national arena, is supposed, among other things, to give effect to. It is hardly surprising, also, that in the same new empirical spirit, Professor Tunkin should charge Soviet jurists, using language oddly reminiscent of the American Legal Realists, with "weakness and incompleteness in juridical argumentation and a tendency to slip into the easier path of ready-made political argumentation reinforced by quotations"; with "dogmatism, . . . the use of citations instead of creative thought, . . . isolation from actual reality".

Professor Tunkin goes on to set as the main goal for the new, post-Stalin, post–Cold War, Soviet science of international law, not merely "knowledge of what exists in international law but active participation in changing it".

Soviet international law, in its new period of maturity thus ushered in, will certainly be empirical and problem-oriented. But it will also, at the same time, inevitably be concerned with recognising, and assisting in the effectuation of, widespread social change in the World Community. When the younger Soviet jurist, Professor R. A. Touzmoukhamedov, who teaches international law at that special university in Moscow set up for students from the "new", Afro-Asian countries, — the Patrice Lumumba Friendship University, — contends that the so-called "wars of national liberation" do not contradict the principles of Soviet-Western Friendly Relations (Peaceful Coexistence); and that the U.N. General Assembly, by adopting the Universal Declaration of Human Rights, gave a form of *de facto* standing to national liberation movements, he serves notice that the Soviet Union has no intention, in spite of the continually extending *détente* with the West, of reneging altogether on its earlier propaganda and also material support for the principles of de-Colonisation and national independence and self-determination. The degree of concrete Soviet implementation and follow-up of such abstract general principles, in terms of actual supply of arms and *matériel* and "volunteers", will, of course, be conditioned by power realities and the dangers of escalation into big-power conflict and nuclear war. But the principles themselves could hardly be abandoned by Soviet political decision-makers without intolerable Soviet loss of face in the "Third World" and without lending further support to Chinese Communist charges as to Soviet ideological "Revisionism". Soviet juridical science can thus be expected to continue to maintain something of an ambivalent, Janus-like attitude, facing at once forward to its assured future as one of the politically great and economically prosperous, industrial civilisations; and also at times backward to its original, revolutionary, Marxist heritage.

It would be foolish for the West, by the same token, to eschew the advantages of its own (in the case of France and of the United States, at least) revolutionary past, and to regard international law today as necessarily synonymous with maintenance of the political *status quo*. The major Western countries have, by now, de-colonised and granted independence and self-government to their former Imperial possessions — in some cases, perhaps, reluctantly and tardily, but in most cases voluntarily and even gracefully. Since no really sophisticated legal system likes to reach a morally absurd result, there would be something rather wrong with modern international law, whether Soviet or Western-based, if it created or maintained or even tolerated legal barriers against full self-determination and political independence for subject peoples. We have referred to the reluctance of many

States, particularly "new" States, in the past to accept the compulsory jurisdiction of the World Court; because those States understood that the World Court would apply "old" rules in whose creation and development they had not themselves participated, and many of which they considered to be unreasonable or unjust. It is on the basis of an asserted dichotomy between international legality and international justice, with the World Court being concerned, by definition, with ascertaining legality and not with justice, that many such States have preferred to resort to direct political action rather than to submit their disputes and complaints to arbitration, compulsory judicial settlement, or other similar forms of institutionally-based international problem-solving. Thus India in 1961 seized, by direct military action, the Portuguese colonial *enclave* within India, of Goa, relying on the political force of the sweeping anti-Colonialist declarations that had been adopted by the U.N. General Assembly in 1960 and subsequently. In effect, the Indian position was that the U.N. General Assembly votes had given some form of collective legitimation to anti-Colonialist actions such as this forcible Indian termination of Portuguese sovereignty over Goa. Though India was cited before the U.N. Security Council for its invasion of Goa, there was no formal Security Council condemnation of its action; and the various Western critics of the Indian action, by declining to take the issue to the U.N. General Assembly, in effect conceded that they could not expect to win, there, a political verdict unfavourable to India. The temptation to other States to follow India's example and to resort to direct action in "anti-Colonialist" situations, wherever they have the military-strategic power to do that and whenever they can reasonably (because of the absence of immediate big-power involvement) expect to get away with it politically, must remain. And this is why it behoves Western political leaders, in place of old-line, essentially negative or defensive, international law positions, to take a more imaginative and forward-looking attitude to the final liquidation of the last surviving remnants of the old Colonial empires. And this is why, also, these same Western political leaders must give prime attention to the problem of effecting and facilitating peaceful change in international law and in the complex of political, social, and economic interests that it exists to serve or to protect.

Likewise, I think Western political leaders must learn the occasional merits of self-restraint in pressing even what they regard as legitimate, legally-based claims. One may doubt, for example, whether it was wise political statecraft for the West to press the issue of U.N. Expenses for reference to the World Court for Advisory Opinion. It was, after all, a high political, or policy, issue of a character that the United States Supreme Court in the past used to prefer to treat as a non-justiciable, "political question". Once the issue of the U.N. Expenses had been referred to the World Court, the opinion of the Court majority, with its undoubted Western juridical background and affiliations, lent an air of definitiveness to the Western-preferred policy solution, making that solution the "legal" one and thus making it difficult or impossible for the Soviet Union to retreat without admitting error and so incurring intolerable loss of face.

There is a dangerous temptation on the part of some Western international lawyers to try to project, too literally and too uncritically, into the World arena, the patterns of legal thought-ways and also legal-institutional organisation that they have grown accustomed to in their own internal legal systems. This is especially true in the case of North American lawyers. We tend to assume that what has worked well in our own national societies — the federal structure, a strong central executive, a policy-making, legislating, Supreme Court — must work equally well or better when translated into the World Community. This is, of course, a form of Anglo-Saxon legal arrogance, reminiscent of the somewhat naive confidence of that one-time U.S. Secretary of Defence who proclaimed that what is good for General Motors is necessarily good for the country. It ignores the essential background societal conditions that have made those special institutional forms politically viable in our own societies — the substantial degree of general popular consensus behind the positive law; and the availability of, and public support for, application of community police power to ensure that executive or judicially-created legal norms are really applied in fact as law-in-action. Such an essentially simplistic approach to the constitutionalism of World Public Order may end up doing great harm to the cause of international law generally by placing impossible political burdens and strains on organs conceived of and designed for essentially more modest political purposes. Insofar as some of these intellectual attitudes and preferences were undoubtedly developed on the part of Western international lawyers at the time of the original Western political dominance in the main United Nations organs, there is also a risk that they may boomerang politically in the new era when United Nations' membership has expanded to near universality and Western power and influence declined in proportion. Though, in fairness to the former U.S. Secretary of State, Dean Acheson, it must be said that he has always taken the long view of international law and relations and avoided the temptations of purely *ad hoc* responses to particular cases, I take it that it is the realisation of these political facts-of-life in the contemporary World Community that accounts for some of the political thrust of Dean Acheson's public criticisms of the U.N. Security Council action of December 16th, 1966, imposing a ban on the buying of key exports from Rhodesia and on the selling of oil to Rhodesia. Dean Acheson assailed the United Nations' action as being an illegal intervention, in violation of Article 2 (4) of the U.N. Charter which obliges all U.N. members to refrain from the threat or use of force against the territorial integrity or political independence of any state.

The U.S. Ambassador to the United Nations, Arthur Goldberg, replied to Dean Acheson's legal arguments, in a speech delivered in Washington to the Association of American Law Schools, on December 29th, 1966. In that part of his speech where he seeks to rest his case on technical legal arguments, Mr. Goldberg is not especially persuasive. Where he argues that the breakaway, Rhodesian government is not a "state" because its establishment is "illegal" vis-à-vis its "legitimate sovereign", Great Britain, Mr. Goldberg uses highly positivistic legal arguments that are rather surprising for an American-trained lawyer. British lawyers themselves have always tended to opt for the "declaratory", and not the "constitutive", theory of state recognition, and to argue that whether a state exists or not is a question of political fact which should be uncluttered by irrelevant moral judgments — a policy that the British Foreign Office applied quite happily in recognising Communist China, in marked contrast to the U.S. State Department's attitude there.

But Ambassador Goldberg speaks with much greater confidence and authority when he defends the Security Council ban, and the United States support for that action, on the broadest policy grounds. In rejecting what he pointedly characterises as the "false and hateful doctrine" of racial superiority, Ambassador Goldberg goes on to contend for an "affirmative" concept of international law:

> What could not be accepted by the United States in the mid-nineteenth century cannot be accepted by the international community in the late-twentieth century. . . .
>
> Law must operate to eliminate discrimination, to assure human rights, to feed the hungry, to educate the ignorant, to raise up the oppressed. It must foster in the international realm the same creative and positive values which nations, at their best, have fulfilled in their own domestic life.

Here we are back, of course, to the core of the debate that we saw, earlier, within the bosom of the World Court in the South-West Africa case judgment of July, 1966. What is the nature and character of contemporary international law? Is it a static pattern of old juridical relationships, or is it a continuing process of creative adjustment of old positive law rules to rapidly changing societal conditions and expectations? What institutional limitations, if any, are imposed on international legal decision-makers, by the terms of their charters and the jurisdictional definitions of their office? Should the legal *honoratiores* follow the course of political prudence and exercise self-restraint; or should they, by contrast, practise activism and assume an affirmative responsibility for trying to re-mould international society in the image of a World Community in continuing revolution? In a word, are what Mr. Justice Frankfurter used to call the "rôles and missions" of the lawyer today to be the Metternichean maintenance of the political-military *status quo* of 1945 and the preservation of a *détente* limited essentially to mutual Soviet-Western self-interest, or can and should the international lawyer strike out boldly and with *élan* to promote, in Pope John XXIII's inspired phrase, an *aggiornamento* of international law and international society, equally?

.   .   .

The question tends to become urgent as the basic patterns of World Public Order that have been dominant in the World Community since the rapid break-up of the victorious wartime coalition after 1945, themselves break down or disintegrate under pressure of rapidly changing World events. I mean here the general condition of Bipolarity and the twin political-military bloc system, Soviet and Western; and the initially uneasy and uncertain political-military balance of power between the two blocs, that itself eventually ripened into the Soviet-Western *détente*, more or less confirming and legitimating the *de facto* post-war territorial settlements effected with the conclusion of hostilities in Europe in the early summer of 1945. The originally hostile Soviet-Western ideological confrontation, and the division of the post-war World into the two great spheres of influence dominated by the two great powers, resulting from the inception of the Cold War, gave way in time to a factual, if not a *juridical*, condition of peaceful coexistence between the two rival social and economic systems, in which the mutual and reciprocal self-interest of the two bloc leaders seemed to emerge as a conservative, and at times even reactionary, force — in the end more concerned with maintaining the immediate political *status quo* than in venturing on political fishing expeditions with unknown and largely unpredictable consequences. If the original, "One World" premise of the United Nations at its inception in 1945, had been shattered by the break-up of the wartime alliance and the rapid onset of the ideological conflict, making the United Nations itself at best a lesser or subordinate arena for resolving international conflicts, it must, in retrospect, be admitted that the era of Bipolarity and the twin bloc system was not so terrible, after all, as it may sometimes have seemed to us when we were actually living through it. The Cold War balance of power between the two blocs, followed by the nuclear balance of terror between them, did succeed in maintaining peace in Central Europe throughout the post-war era and in avoiding a global conflagration, albeit at the cost of many grave local injustices. It gave way, in time, to a highly developed and nuanced system of inter-bloc law, founded on tacit agreements or understandings between the two blocs as to observance of Cold War minimum ground rules, — for example, the mutual acceptance of bloc territorial integrity, and of non-intervention of each bloc *inter se*; the renunciation of total (nuclear) war as an instrument of political change, as between the two blocs; the limitation, as far as possible, of the membership of the Nuclear Club, and the restriction of the decision-making power as to use of nuclear weapons or as to recourse to nuclear war.

It was, after all, the Soviet Union's clear indication, in 1959, to the Chinese Communist government that the 1957 Soviet-Chinese military aid agreement did not mean that Communist China would be equipped by the Soviet Union with nuclear weapons, that began the present Sino-Soviet dispute. The Peking government decided, then and there, to develop nuclear weapons under its own steam; the immediate consequence was that, in July of 1960, the Soviet Union withdrew its army of officers, technicians, scientists, and other development advisers from China, with resultant catastrophic effects on the economic re-building of China. The blow to Communist China was so sudden that the Chinese leaders charged that Soviet Premier Khrushchev had betrayed the Chinese ideological revolution.

To the Cold War minimum ground rules already mentioned we may add the avoidance of "surprise" or sudden change in the inter-bloc balance of power, lest surprise itself should provoke an irrational, nuclear reaction on the part of the other side; the exercise of economy in the use of power, that is of military force or direct action, in inter-bloc relations. These Cold War "rules of the game", resting as they so obviously did on mutuality and reciprocity of interest as between the two blocs and their leaders, did much to fill the gap in international security arrangements constituted by the absence of any one comprehensive, or universal, system of World Public Order and by the failure of the United Nations organisation successfully to maintain its original "One World" image or to assert its place as the really significant arena for international problem-solving. However primitive, institutionally, Bipolarity and the twin bloc system may have been, viewed as a form of international peace-keeping arrangements, it did reflect more or less accurately the facts of the post-World War II World power structure; it did recognise the necessary minimum relation between international law and power; and it did, in the end, succeed experientially, in that it did, after all, maintain World peace and prevent nuclear conflict.

Paradoxically, as the system of Bipolarity attained its *apogée* with the rapid achievement, concretisation, and extension, of the Soviet-Western *détente* in the Khrushchev-Kennedy era and beyond that, it was seen to have in it the seeds of its own decay. Proportionately as the Soviet-Western, inter-bloc, understanding increased and deepened, the degree of internal cohesion and discipline and cooperation within each bloc, Soviet and Western, weakened and declined. And so the situation has been reached today where the two political-military blocs, NATO and the Warsaw Pact, are in internal disarray and even confusion, as the threat of nuclear war between the two bloc leaders, the Soviet Union and the United States, has largely receded into history; and with it the need, or indeed the power, of the two bloc leaders effectively to crack the whip over political-military satellites or associates.

The internal schisms within the two blocs, and the beginning of political de-polarisation in the World Community as the Cold War has ended in its nuclear, and perhaps also its more general ideological, phase, constitute in themselves what President de Gaulle has described as the "end of the post-war period in Europe". If the necessarily larger number of states that must now be consulted for purposes of any effective international law norms, resting both on genuine inter-systems consensus and on the new facts of power in the contemporary World Community, makes the process of securing such international agreement so much more difficult or at least complex today, it must be conceded that, by way of compensation, the removal of the threat of nuclear war and of direct big power, Soviet-U.S., hostile military confrontation in Europe, has immensely facilitated the task of securing a final peace settlement in Europe; and of solving some old problems like establishing a nuclear-free zone athwart Central Europe, and resolving the Berlin crisis and the two Germanies issue, and settling the territorial frontiers and the matter of the various "irredentist" claims in Central and Eastern Europe. These are some of the positive factors in the new pluralistic World Community that now seems to be succeeding to the old twin bloc system of the era of Bipolarity. The possibility of a united, or at least of an economically, culturally, and even politically integrated Europe, on supra-national lines, transcending the old post-war ideological divisions, now opens up before us. And though, in the Gaullist vision, it may have seemed at times to be hostile to both U.S. and Soviet demands or pretensions to political hegemony within the bloc, in the long run the creation of such a strengthened and cohesive Europe, allied to the practical *détente* and indeed the increasingly active cooperation between the Soviet Union and the United States, means, in effect, a North Hemisphere bloc — of the Soviet Union, the United States, Europe, plus Japan — sharing a common industrial civilisation and advanced technology, and united, on the whole, as to the common minimum principles of World Public Order.

·   ·   ·

The sharp welling of Afro-Asian resentment over the World Court majority decision, in July, 1966, in the South-West Africa case, is another reminder of the truth, already recognised by perceptive students of international law and relations, that the sharpest divisions and conflicts of the last third of the century are going to be, not between the Soviet bloc and the West, but between the highly industrialised, technologically advanced, economically well-to-do, countries, which include, equally, the United States and its main allies, and the Soviet Union and its European associates; and the economically under-privileged rest of the World. The old East-West (Soviet-Western) conflicts of the Cold War era are, as President de Gaulle seems to have been the first among Western political leaders to have recognised, increasingly being replaced by a new North-South geographical division in which the differentiation is one, markedly, of relative standards of living and of economic and physical well-being generally.

It is becoming clear that the achievement and maintenance of a viable system of World Public Order, during the last third of the century, will depend in large measure on narrowing the gap, in terms of community well-being, between the Soviet bloc countries and the West on the one hand, and the Third World of the Afro-Asian, emergent countries, on the other. At the moment, the disparity between the economically privileged, and the economically under-privileged, countries, is increasing all the time, because of the extraordinary technological advances that continue to be made all the time in the former group.

Recognition of the common, Soviet bloc and Western, interest in promoting economic and social development through strengthened bilateral and multilateral cooperation, was decisive in launching the United Nations Decade of Development. President Kennedy, in his speech to the U.N. General Assembly on September 25th, 1961, rightly recognised that economic development could become a cooperative, Soviet bloc *and* Western — and not a competitive, Soviet bloc *versus* Western — enterprise. The U.N. General Assembly, at its 16th session, responded to President Kennedy's appeal by designating the current decade as the Development Decade, with an official target, for the end of the decade in 1970, of a minimum annual growth of five per cent in the national incomes of the less developed countries, to be achieved by means of United Nations-sponsored technical assistance, regional surveys, pilot projects, and other programmes for promoting economic growth.

One very concrete, institutionally-based, United Nations' effort for achieving this, has been the United Nations Conference on Trade and Development, or UNCTAD as it came to be known by trade officials around the world. UNCTAD was called into being by the United Nations Economic and Social Council, at the initiative of the less developed countries which had laid the groundwork for it in meetings of U.N. regional commissions and special committees in Latin America, Asia and Africa. In a Joint Declaration of 77 Developing Countries, made at the conclusion of the UNCTAD conference in June, 1964, the conference itself was described as a "significant step towards creating a new and just world economic order".

The central purpose of UNCTAD was to consider ways of bridging the so-called Prebisch Gap, named after the conference's own secretary-general. This is the gap between what it is estimated that the developing countries will need in foreign exchange to finance their import requirements for development, and what it is estimated that they are likely to earn in foreign exchange from their export of primary goods. UNCTAD

Secretary-General Prebisch himself, however, estimated that by 1970 this gap would reach 20 billion dollars per year, assuming imports sufficient to support the five per cent annual growth target for national income laid down by the United Nations General Assembly for the Decade for Development. And even if half this gap could be filled by foreign aid, it would still, according to Dr. Prebisch's estimate, leave about 10 billion dollars that would have to be financed through increased exports by the less developed countries.

UNCTAD itself provided a clear confrontation between the rich, predominantly white, states of the Northern Hemisphere (both Soviet bloc and Western), and the poorer, predominantly non-white, states of the Southern hemisphere. For the first time, a really coherent and organised, developing countries' lobby appeared, comprising the originally 75, and later 77, Latin American, Asian, and African countries represented at the conference. The 77 met and caucused together, and they chose to negotiate through common spokesmen. They also voted as a bloc, in order to bring pressure to bear on the industrialised nations. UNCTAD was thus the first major international conference in which the conventional East-West, Soviet-Western, confrontation that had characterised international relations throughout the old, Cold War era, was replaced by the new North-South alignment.

The sheer weight of numbers of the 77 developing countries caused fears on the part of the minority, Northern hemisphere, states that resolutions might be forced through without regard to the feelings of this minority of states that would, after all, inevitably be called on to bear the main economic burdens of the majority decisions and recommendations. The Western countries had originally urged a 40-member Trade and Development Board, responsible to the U.N. General Assembly, on which 14 seats would be Western, with 10 permanent; and in which, also, a collective veto would operate. The final conclusion of the conference, however, was in favour of a 55-member Board, with 18 seats for the West, 22 for the Afro-Asian countries, 9 for Latin America, and 6 for the Soviet bloc; and with voting to be by simple majority. In general, in terms of the UNCTAD proposals and recommendations, industrial countries are called on to impose a standstill on trade barriers to the main commodity exports of developing countries, and also to reduce internal taxes and to broaden quotas.

It would be easy to say that the U.N. Decade of Development and UNCTAD itself provide both the goals, and also a structural base, for a more equitable world economic order. The fact is, however, that the Resolution of the U.N. General Assembly at its 16th session, inaugurating the Decade of Development, set an exceedingly modest goal in looking to attainment of a five per cent accrual of national income in the developing countries, by 1970. As the leading Czech jurist, Professor Rudolf Bystricky, points out, even if this aim were attained, it would mean 100 dollars per capita income, per annum, at the most,— by all standards, a minimal individual income. Dr. Bystricky's own solution, in part, for bridging the gap between the economically privileged and the economically under-privileged countries, is to require the former Colonial powers to pay financial compensation to their former Colonial territories. As Professor Bystricky explains, the imposition of such an obligation of compensation upon the former Colonial powers would be:

> for the exploitation and depradation of their natural wealths, for the immense losses caused by the deformation of their economies, and for the plunging of the populations of the former colonial nations into unheard-of misery.

Professor Bystricky draws on his own considerable reputation as a Marxist theorist and international lawyer, to urge that such a duty of financial compensation on the part of the former colonial powers exists as a legal obligation imposed under international law itself. Dr. Bystricky is also highly critical of the final decisions of the United Nations Conference on Trade and Development of 1964, blaming the fact that "no universal autonomous organisation for international trade was created but only an auxiliary organ of the General Assembly", on the postulate of weighted voting which had been raised by the Western States at the conference, allegedly in the fear that they might be outvoted by the overwhelming numbers of the developing countries.

While the remedy advanced by Professor Bystricky might

Université d'Ottawa
Social Sciences Sociales
University of Ottawa

seem as politically drastic as it is certainly (in international law terms) legally novel, it may be doubted whether, even if adopted, it would really be too significant, in purely economic terms, in bridging the economic gap between the developing countries on the one hand and the advanced industrial states on the other. Nor can the tentative steps taken in terms of the U.N. Decade of Development and also UNCTAD be regarded as much more, really, than a promising beginning. And so that "margin of misery" between rich countries (Soviet bloc and Western) and poor countries, continues to be perhaps the really major problem of World Public Order of the last third of the century. It is this that renders really urgent the further concretisation and the further extension of the Soviet-Western *détente*; and also the transition on from the Peaceful Coexistence of the Soviet bloc and West, to a form of much more active, activist, Soviet-Western international cooperation so as to permit joint, Soviet bloc and Western-sponsored, programmes for massive economic development aid and assistance to the vast under-privileged mass of the World.

For the whole record of Soviet-Western relations, since the political event of the October Revolution of 1917, shows that what may once have appeared to be irreconcilable, life-and-death, conflicts over ultimate goals or objectives of society, have frequently been no more than disagreements or differences as to means or machinery for concretely attaining human welfare and social betterment. The old, Soviet-based *ideological* revolution has, in this sense, increasingly given way to or been displaced by the contemporary *technological* revolution in which the prime concern has been with improving and perfecting the scientific methods and techniques of an advanced industrial civilisation, and in which, in consequence, the historical development of Soviet society has increasingly paralleled, and in no substantial sense conflicted with, that of Western society. There is reason to believe that, with properly-based, joint Soviet and Western, development aid programmes, this technological revolution can be successfully exported to the "new" countries, with consequent general gain throughout the World Community in terms of rapidly rising standards of political and economic well-being of all mankind. If we cannot — the Soviet Union and

ourselves — cooperate in successfully exporting our own technological revolutions to the developing countries, then the
old-fashioned and simplistic, anachronistic throwback to 1917,
of the ideological revolution, remains as a "brooding omni-
presence in the sky", — a sort of universal panacea for all political,
social, and economic ills of the contemporary World Community,
with ample enough forces available and ready to use and exploit
it in the interests of non-peaceful change and of the redress, by
violence if need be, of the ever-accentuating imbalance, as to
wealth and well-being, between the economically prosperous
and the economically backward, halves of the World.

Université d'Ottawa
Social Sciences Sociales
University of Ottawa

Bibliothèque ersité d'Ottawa **Échéance**		The Library University of Ottawa **Date due**